MORE OF PAUL HARVEY'S
THE REST OF THE STORY

MORE OF PAUL HARVEY'S

THE REST OF THE STORY

by Paul Aurandt

EDITED AND COMPILED
BY LYNNE HARVEY

William Morrow and Company, Inc.
New York   1980

Library of Congress Cataloging in Publication Data

Aurandt, Paul.
    More of Paul Harvey's The rest of the story.

    1. History, Modern—Anecdotes, facetiae, satire,
etc.   2. United States—History—Anecdotes,
facetiae, satire, etc.   I. Harvey, Lynne.
II. Title.   III. Title: Rest of the story.
D210.A83   909.08   80-10665
ISBN 0-688-03669-4

Printed in the United States of America

First Edition

1   2   3   4   5   6   7   8   9   10

Contents

7

Contents

We laugh, we cry, we are born, we die,
Who will riddle me the *how* and the *why*?
—ALFRED LORD TENNYSON

MORE OF PAUL HARVEY'S
THE REST
OF THE STORY

1. The Light Show

On the night of April 14, the ocean liner *Californian* has progressed to within fifteen hundred miles of her destination, Boston Harbor.

Midnight.

Second Officer Herbert Stone is due for watch on the bridge.

Reporting for duty, Stone finds his apprentice seaman glued to a pair of binoculars, staring toward the black horizon.

He, the apprentice, has sighted a steamer in the distance.

He can make out the ship's masthead light, her red light, and a glare of white lights on her afterdeck.

Stone asks the apprentice to try for communication by means of the *Californian*'s Morse lamp.

A bright beacon signal is flashed.

No answer from the steamer.

"Will that be all, sir?"

Stone nods; the apprentice leaves to make record in the patent log.

Now Second Officer Stone is alone on the bridge.

Glancing idly over the water, a white flash catches his eye—a white flash of light in the direction of the distant steamer.

Stone scratches his head, picks up the binoculars. Four more white flashes, like skyrockets bursting in the heavens.

Stone notifies the ship's captain.

Over the voice pipe, the captain asks if the flashes appeared to be company signals.

Stone cannot say for sure.

The captain then requests further communication attempt through the Morse lamp.

By now Stone's apprentice has returned to the bridge.

The beacon signal is employed once more.

Still no answer from the steamer.

Lifting the binoculars to his eyes once more, Stone observes three more flashes in the continuing light show, but now his attention is drawn to the steamer's cabin lights.

They seem to be disappearing, as though the steamer were sailing away.

At 1:40 A.M., Stone sees the eighth and last white flash in the night sky.

In one hour, all the steamer's lights have vanished into the blackness.

It is not until 4:00 A.M. that anyone on board the liner *Californian* learns THE REST OF THE STORY.

Neither the Captain nor the Second Officer aboard the *Californian* had interpreted the white skyrocket flashes as cause for alarm.

It was a matter of coincidence that they had been seen in the first place. For earlier that night—the night of April 14—the *Californian* had reversed engines and parked as a precautionary measure, halted in her course by an immense field of oceanic ice.

That unscheduled stop in the middle of the sea had provided the *Californian* a ringside seat for an unimaginable drama.

The distant steamer had intended those rocket flares as distress signals, and the *Californian*—only nine miles away —might have rushed to her aid.

Except for one thing. The steamer was sending other distress calls—by radio. And the *Californian* was well within range of those messages.

But her radio operator was asleep.

The *Californian*'s fledgling radio operator—fresh from training school—was fast asleep in his cabin. And that night the ship's Second Officer, from his vantage point on the bridge, unwittingly watched the sinking . . . of the *Titanic*.

2. Excuses, Excuses!

Mrs. Paul is the choir director for the West Side Baptist Church in Beatrice, Nebraska.

Her daughter, Marilyn, is the church pianist.

Neither has ever been late for choir practice; to the contrary, both are in the habit of arriving fifteen minutes early.

It's Wednesday evening, March 1, 1950—seven o'clock.

Choir practice begins at seven-thirty.

Mrs. Paul calls to her daughter upstairs: They should be leaving now. It's almost time.

No answer.

Mrs. Paul returns to her last-minute preparation.

And the minutes are ticking away.

It is 7:15 P.M. when she realizes—her daughter is asleep. So Mrs. Paul goes upstairs, awakens her daughter. There is time only to tidy up and start out.

This will be the first time either Mrs. Paul or her daughter Marilyn has ever been late for choir practice. Their perfect attendance record is broken.

But you know what?

There are eighteen members in the West Side Baptist Church Choir, and each and every one—that very same night—is also late for practice!

All eighteen have perfectly valid excuses, and all are late.

You've heard the excuse of Mrs. Paul, the choir director: Her daughter Marilyn, the church pianist, had fallen asleep after dinner and did not awaken in time.

But the others had excuses, too.

Ladona Vandegrift, a high school sophomore, was having trouble with her homework. Like Mrs. Paul and her daughter, Miss Vandegrift knew practice began promptly —and she always came early—but this evening she was detained by a particularly baffling geometry problem.

17

Royena Estes and her sister Sadie were ready to leave their house on time. But their car wouldn't start. So the two sisters called Miss Vandegrift and asked her to pick them up. Miss Vandegrift was working on her geometry, remember, and the Estes sisters had to wait.

Ordinarily, Mrs. Schuster was ten minutes early for choir practice. The night of March 1 she was detained at her mother's house. The two were preparing for a later missionary meeting.

Herb Kipf was at his own home—would have been early, too. But there was this important letter he had to write. He had been putting it off for some time. The time got away from him.

Excuses, excuses.

Joyce Black would probably not have been early. She would have been on time, though. It was just so cold out that evening, she wanted to stay in the house until the last possible minute. So she was late.

Harvey Ahl would have been on time, but his wife was out of town. That left him in charge of their two young sons. A friend had invited Harvey and the two boys out to dinner. A pleasant conversation carried them away, and Harvey was late.

Lucille Jones and Dorothy Wood were high school girls, lived next door to each other. Lucille was listening to a half-hour radio program that began at seven o'clock. She just *had* to hear how it ended. Dorothy waited for her.

Pastor Klempel and his wife were always on time for choir practice. Not the evening of March 1, however. Pastor Klempel's wristwatch—the accuracy of which he was always so proud—that night, five minutes slow.

The remaining choir members had equally valid excuses for their tardiness. Excuses, excuses—eighteen in all.

Never before nor since had each and every choir member of the West Side Baptist Church been late for choir practice on the same evening. That was Wednesday, March

1, 1950—choir practice scheduled as usual for 7:30 P.M.

No one showed up at 7:30. That is THE REST OF THE STORY.

Seven-thirty P.M. was the time when a natural-gas leak —surfacing in the basement of the West Side Baptist Church—was ignited by the furnace.

The church blew up, was demolished.

The old furnace of the West Side Baptist Church was directly below the choir loft.

The *empty* choir loft.

3. You Can't Come Inside

Country singer Lonzo Green was a stranger in town that summer. He had brought his wife and two children all the way from Cherry Valley, Arkansas, to visit relatives in Tennessee.

But, as I say, he was a stranger in town, unaccustomed to the local customs and taboos. So Lonzo was a bit surprised to learn that a friend of his young nephew was under no circumstances to be allowed in the house.

His teen-age nephew Jimmy had proudly, excitedly, spread the word around school that Uncle Lonzo had come to town and was staying with them, right there in the apartment on Lauderdale Court!

Naturally this impressed Jimmy's young friends, especially one—a quiet, dark-haired boy of fifteen.

Jimmy came home that day and told Lonzo about the boy, how he had his own guitar but he didn't know how to tune it. If Lonzo would just tune the guitar for him, the boy would be very grateful.

Lonzo said he'd be happy to oblige and asked Jimmy when his friend could come with his guitar.

Jimmy's eager smile fell. His friend could come by that afternoon, but Mom and Dad had made it a firm rule that the boy was not allowed inside. He was from the wrong side of the tracks, they'd explained, and some folks called him "white trash." Perhaps he could meet Lonzo outside, but he was not to be permitted in the house.

Lonzo didn't quite understand but he nodded, said nothing, and a couple of hours later he walked out into the sunlight and waited.

In a minute or two, a figure appeared at the end of the lane, a boy with dark hair, a battered guitar slung across his back.

As the boy walked closer, Lonzo studied the sensitive features, the timid sidewise glances at this better neighborhood, the sting of self-consciousness. Then he noticed that the boy's guitar, obviously inexpensive, doubtless secondhand, was tethered by a piece of string.

They met at the curb, shook hands. The youngster gave a shy slight smile—and there, at the curbside, they sat down.

Lonzo took the instrument from the boy. Had no one ever shown him how to tune his guitar?

The answer came in a soft, polite Southern drawl: "No, sir."

Lonzo demonstrated, placing his fingers over the proper frets. The boy watched intently. After the guitar was tuned, he thanked Lonzo and began to rise from the curb.

But Lonzo would not let him leave. He had tasted poverty in his own youth; he too had known the other side of the neighborhood barrier which separated "acceptable" from "unacceptable" people. How much a little kindness from the right person would have meant back then!

So Lonzo asked the dark-haired boy to stay a while longer.

The hesitant smile broke into a broad grin.

With the boy's guitar, Lonzo played and sang a familiar hill country ballad . . . then another . . . and another. Shortly the haunting reticence in the boy's eyes was gone, replaced by the joy of the music.

Cars streamed past them. The shadows of late afternoon grew long. After Lonzo had taught the boy to play a few chords on the guitar, the youngster thanked him again and was on his way.

He was not invited inside. Not then.

Lonzo Green would never meet him again.

But the boy had left his company with a warm memory, a memory he would carry throughout the remarkable, radical changes in his own life.

For someday, you would invite the dark-haired boy from the wrong side of town into your home.

And when he crossed those tracks for good he brought with him his guitar, the soft polite drawl, the hesitant smile.

That was twenty-nine summers . . . and thirty-three motion pictures . . . and four hundred million records . . . and a lifetime ago.

And if there is a happy ending, mixed in with our own bittersweet memories, it is that the boy was never, ever after, unwelcome again.

The young fellow who once upon a time couldn't come inside was Elvis Presley.

And now you know THE REST OF THE STORY.

4. Great Expectations

If today it is often true, a hundred and fifty years ago it was invariably so. The hopes of a family rested on the male child.

Parents and daughters all sacrificed to promote the son; if there were more than one, the eldest.

A century and a half ago, Patrick's family lived in a tiny village in Yorkshire, the north of England.

Patrick, the father, was vicar of the village church. His wife died young; his brood included three daughters and a son. Just one son—named Branwell.

Branwell was considered the family genius.

At an early age, he demonstrated remarkable artistic and literary talents. His drawing and paintings, his poetry and prose, seemed to forecast a brilliant future for whichever he chose.

At first, Branwell favored art. His family—his father and three sisters—scrimped and saved and sent him off to London to study at the Royal Academy of Arts.

In a few weeks, Branwell returned home penniless and without the education for which he had been sponsored.

Yet the family confidence remained undimmed.

Branwell was merely misunderstood, they said. What he needed was the opportunity to work, to develop on his own the genius with which he was obviously endowed.

The family—the father, the three sisters—found a position for Branwell as a private tutor. Surely that would give him enough spare time to paint and to write.

And once again, Branwell returned home, no job, no money. Only excuses.

As the excuses piled up, as one failure led to another and another, Branwell's delinquent recreation expanded to include alcohol—eventually opium—and his already

23

unpromising situation was made even less promising than before.

Still, his sisters were certain that Branwell would one day be recognized, universally acclaimed as the genius he was. Inspired by this earnest hope for their brilliant brother, they continued to work to support him.

The sisters cut corners on household expenses; they hired themselves out as teachers and governesses.

What came of their great expectations is THE REST OF THE STORY.

Today, one hundred and fifty years later, no one looks at Branwell's paintings; no one reads anything he wrote.

He died as he lived, an unmitigated failure. The devoted, concerted efforts of Branwell's three sisters were, in this respect, in vain. They had labored to finance their brother's dreams and eventually his excesses, for nothing.

But as Branwell's three sisters sought to relieve the dull drudgery of their own hard, narrow lives, they—in their only spare time, usually by candlelight in the dark of night—tried to emulate the lofty literary ability they believed was their brother's.

So far as we know, their brother had no such literary ability.

But *they* did.

For the three sisters who flattered and supported Branwell with their unfailing confidence, the three young women who unselfishly invested their all in their brother, were Anne and Emily and Charlotte.

Anne wrote the novel *Agnes Grey*.

And Emily penned the classic *Wuthering Heights*.

And Charlotte authored the immortal *Jane Eyre*.

Anne, Emily and Charlotte—Brontë.

5. Warners' Number One

He was a big name in silent films, starred in nearly forty. And if he enjoyed more so-called star treatment than others in his studio, you'll understand why.

Only minor hardships accompanied his special celebrity: boring premieres, long promotional tours, hospital visits, openings.

But the other side of the coin was shiny.

While other cast members had to work in sometimes miserable weather, his studio contract provided for a stand-in. While his co-stars were largely neglected and underpaid, he was given all consideration and was making a fortune.

As one might expect, the sense of this preferential regard was measured in dollars and cents.

During the Silent Era, he was Warner Bros.' biggest star. He was the mainstay of the studio's financial structure. On several occasions, when it seemed Warners might go under, the box-office gross of this one performer brought in sufficient revenue to pay other losses —losses on such films as those starring John Barrymore.

In motion picture plots, this hero always "saved the day." In real life also.

Here's a story line for you. Old-time mining town, lots of rough characters. Our hero, in order to pass through town unnoticed, is wearing a false beard. Predictably the beard falls off, our hero is recognized, and at once he is fleeing an angry lynch mob.

Stale as it sounds, this was the sort of bread-and-butter silent movie plot that kept Warner Bros.' books in the black.

The star of that particular movie served as a cornerstone for more than three dozen others like it.

He was Warners' top star. In 1926, he superseded Chaplin and Valentino and Fairbanks in the polls. In that pre-Oscar era, he was voted most popular film performer of the year.

Did public relations people have private problems with this celebrity? Press releases made him out to be everything nice and kind and considerate. Good to his mother, fond of children and all that.

Actually Warners' Number One was the most temperamental star in Hollywood. His scraps with upstagers, minor cast members and well-meaning directors were legendary within the industry. He never drank but seemed to achieve the same raucous result without drinking.

Yet any indiscretion was promptly forgiven. For this was the star who more than once saved Warner Bros., the performer whose personal box-office popularity bailed them out when others were losing money.

At the height of his popularity he received twelve thousand fan letters a week. He even had Darryl F. Zanuck for a scriptwriter.

Warners' Number One, the temperamental star who won the hearts of a nation, the most popular matinee idol of 1926, the performer who kept Warner Bros. in the black, carrying that studio safely into the age of the "talkies"—was himself unable to talk.

He was a German Shepherd named Rin Tin Tin.

And the false beard?

They were attempting to disguise him as a wolf!

Now you know THE REST OF THE STORY.

6. If

When rape results in pregnancy, or when giving birth might cost the mother's life, few women would fail to consider as an alternative:

Abortion.

But let's say you're a doctor—a physician not morally adverse to terminating a patient's pregnancy—and the circumstances are neither frivolous nor dire.

Let's say that on a given day you are consulted by two young women, both pregnant, both doubtful as to whether they should be.

Now, remember: such a choice is ultimately the mother's, but because you are a physician, and because your judgment is respected, and because your patient is seeking guidance, everything you say, regardless of how clinically objective—yes, even the tone of your voice—may sway her decision.

Yours is a position of enormous responsibility. Like it or not, the very expression on your face could save or extinguish a life.

Your first expectant mother is Caterina.

Caterina is unmarried, obviously in her teens, obviously poor.

You ask her age, and she tells you, and at once you realize she has overstated her years by one or two or three.

Caterina is in the first trimester of her pregnancy.

You ask if she has been pregnant before.

Caterina shakes her head.

Studying her, you wonder.

You inquire of her general health; no problems, she says.

And the health of the father?

Caterina shrugs; her eyes fall.

She has lost contact with the father of her unborn child. All she knows is he was twenty-three, a lawyer or a notary or something like that. He lives nearby, she thinks; she is not sure. The affair was over quickly, little more than a one-night stand. No child was expected—nor now is it wanted.

What, Doctor, is your advice?

Later the same day, you are consulted by a second expectant mother.

Her name is Klara.

Klara is twenty-eight, married three years, the wife of a government worker; she has the look of a woman accustomed to anguish.

Concerned for the ultimate health of her unborn, Klara explains that for each year of her marriage she has had a child—and each has died; the first within thirty-one months, the second within sixteen months, the third within several days.

Disease? you ask.

Klara nods. She suspects that any future child would be equally susceptible. For you see, her husband is also her second cousin. Both Catholic, they received papal dispensation to marry—though now Klara questions their wisdom in asking permission.

And there's something else . . .

One of Klara's sisters is a hunchback; another sister, the mother of a hunchback.

Klara is in the first trimester of her fourth pregnancy. The odds are against the health of her child. Time is running out.

And it is only later that you learn—Klara's husband is not, as she has said, her second cousin. He is her uncle.

So what, Doctor, is your advice?

In addition to all immediate considerations—physical, moral, religious—the dilemma of whether to terminate a pregnancy is a philosophical question:

Might this life, if left to live, affect the consciousness or even the destiny of mankind?

Yet if the profundity of this question is diminished by the balance which governs all life, there is evidence in the two true stories you have just heard: the unwed mother with unwanted child; the married mother with the graves of three infants behind her.

For if you, as the hypothetical physician, have opted in both cases for abortion—then you have respectively denied the world the multifaceted genius of Leonardo da Vinci— and spared humanity the terror of Adolf Hitler.

They are THE REST OF THE STORY.

7. Eulogy for an Owl

His name was Walter Elias, a city boy by birth, the son of a building contractor.

Before Walter was five, his parents moved from Chicago to a farm near Marceline, Missouri. And it was there on the farm that Walter would have his first encounter with death.

Walter was only seven that particular lazy summer afternoon not much different from other afternoons. Dad was tending to farm chores, Mother was in the house.

It was the perfect day for a young fellow to go exploring.

Now just beyond a grove of graceful willows was an apple orchard. There Walter could make-believe to his heart's content: that he was lost, which he never was, or that he had captured a wild animal, which he never had.

But today was different.

Directly in front of him, about thirty feet away, perched in the low-drooping branch of an apple tree and apparently sound asleep—was an owl.

The boy froze.

He remembered his father telling him that owls rested during the day so they could hunt by night. What a wonderful pet that funny little bird would make. If only Walter could approach it without awakening it, and snatch it from the tree.

With each step, the lad winced to hear dry leaves and twigs crackle beneath his feet. The owl did not stir.

Closer . . . and closer . . . and at last young Walter was standing under the limb just within range of his quarry.

Slowly he reached up with one hand and grabbed the bird by its legs. He had captured it!

But the owl, waking suddenly, came alive like no other animal Walter had ever seen! In a flurry of beating wings, wild eyes and frightened cries it struggled against the boy's grasp. Walter, stunned, held on.

Now it's difficult to imagine how what happened next, happened. Perhaps the response was sparked by gouging talons or by fear itself. But at some point the terrified boy, still clinging to the terrified bird, flung it to the ground—and stomped it to death.

When it was over, a disbelieving Walter gazed down at the broken heap of bronze feathers and blood. And he cried.

Walter ran from the orchard but later returned to bury the owl, the little pet he would never know. Each shovelful of earth from the shallow grave was moistened with tears of deep regret. And for months thereafter, the owl visited Walter's dreams.

Ashamed, he would tell no one of the incident until many years later. By then, the world forgave him.

For that sad and lonely summer's day in the early spring of Walter Elias brought with it an awakening of the meaning of life.

Walter never, ever again, killed a living creature.

Although all the boyhood promises could not bring that one little owl back to life, through its death a whole world of animals came into being.

For it was then that a grieving seven-year-old boy, attempting to atone for a thoughtless misdeed, first sought to possess the animals of the forest while allowing them to run free—by drawing them.

Now the boy too is gone, but his drawings live on in the incomparable, undying art of Walter Elias . . . Disney.

Walt Disney.

And now you know THE REST OF THE STORY.

8. The Almost-Midshipman

Such is the romance of the sea, its appeal especially to the young, that small boys still dream of running off to join the Navy.

And so did this one boy.

His big brother had been a Navy man, had many exciting recollections of his service. Occasionally brother's Navy comrades were dinner guests, and what stories they told!

Reliving their adventures through countless all-but-sleepless nights, the small boy grew impatiently into his teens.

Now of suitable age to enlist in the armed forces, he discussed the matter with his big brother, received only encouragement. Perhaps, with brother's help, the boy might enter officer's training—might go into the Navy as a midshipman aboard a real Navy war vessel!

It was a thrilling prospect. All that remained was to convince the boy's mother.

The proposal was greeted with a heavy sigh. Mother had bravely accepted all the challenges in her life: the loss of her husband only five years before, the difficulty of rearing more than a half dozen young ones all by herself. And here was yet another challenge, to give up the teen-ager she still perceived as her baby.

Mother, brave once more, gave her consent. The boy might enlist in the Navy if he wished.

And he did.

Surely this was the happiest time heretofore of the young fellow's life, a joyous drama full of glitter and grandeur and great expectations.

Scene Two:

The boy is standing before his mother in a dashing midshipman's uniform. He is bidding her farewell. His belongings are already aboard ship, and the vessel is ready to sail. Good-bye, he tells his mother. He will miss her.

That's when it happened. In an unexpected and uncharacteristic outpouring of emotion, mother began to sob.

This woman, who had already endured so much heartache, now refused to endure any more. Her son must not board that ship. He must not go into the Navy. He must stay and be strong for the rest of his family—especially for her.

Big brother was there, trying to persuade Mother of the Navy's virtues.

The teen-ager in the midshipman's uniform was silent for a long while. Then he spoke:

He did so want a Navy career for himself—but not if it meant bearing the memory of his mother's grief. Much as it disappointed him, he would return his uniform, would order his belongings ashore.

Of all the young men who might have left home in search of adventure and did not—of this world's many almost-midshipmen—the boy you have just met was just one more.

Yet how might any other decision, on his behalf, have affected the Revolutionary War? That is THE REST OF THE STORY.

We owe a mother's eleventh-hour anxiety—for preventing one young man from ascending through the ranks of the British Navy—a boy of fifteen, handsomely clad, bags packed and on board, prepared to embark on quite a different adventure than that for which you remember him.

A boy of fifteen. His name . . . George Washington.

9. Vicky

Vicky wanted a room of her own.

She was a big girl now, she argued. But she did not feel like one. Not with Mommy sleeping in the same room.

It seemed as though there was always a fuss about whether the light should be lit. And why she should wear these slippers or that nightdress. And especially—when she should be put to bed.

And while she was at it, Vicky complained, there was another thing or two.

Must Mommy *always* be holding her hand? Everywhere that Vicky went it seemed that there was Mommy—or some grown-up of whom Mommy approved—holding her hand, making her feel like a baby.

And one thing more . . .

Why was Vicky never allowed to visit with anyone alone? Was Mommy afraid that one of Vicky's friends might steal her away?

She had no privacy, no time to herself, especially when she wanted it the most—at night while she slept.

Vicky wanted a room of her own.

Of course, all of Vicky's protestations were silent ones.

Long ago she had learned that arguing with Mommy was not only futile but an invitation to admonition.

So Vicky kept her complaints to herself, resigned to the feeling that she would always be smothered by Mother.

Hers was a valid complaint. Vicky really was a big girl: she was eighteen years old!

Still, everywhere she went, there was Mother, clutching at her, holding her hand.

Friends, confidantes, other young girls with whom she might share her secret hopes and apprehensions—out of the question. Long ago Mother had decided that for Vicky to be left alone with anyone—for a solitary activity to go unsupervised—would be improper.

For Vicky the most difficult part of all was not having a room of her own. Eighteen years old and still sleeping with Mother, still at the mercy of when *she* would put out the light, when *she* would have Vicky go to sleep.

Those years of Mother-smothering had engendered rebellion. As a child Vicky was given to outbursts of rage— shrieking, stamping tantrums. Once, in a fit of frustration, Vicky threw a pair of sharp scissors at her governess.

Older now, although no less under surveillance and no less frustrated by it, Vicky had calmed down. Quietly she resolved that someday, somehow, she would have that for which she had hoped the longest—her own room—a place to retire quietly each night, and perhaps each day for cherished moments of solitude.

Three and a half weeks after her eighteenth birthday, Vicky got her wish. Her uncle died, and then she got a room of her own.

Forever after, her demonstrative, overprotective mother would remain at a comfortable distance.

It was a joy mixed with remorse because, as she knew, the price of her privacy coincided with the death of an uncle.

But it was *then* she got a room of her own.

And, incidentally, a throne.

Her uncle died and Vicky, at eighteen, became Queen Victoria.

And now you know THE REST OF THE STORY.

10. The Lost Years of Liu Shih-kun

April 1958—the First International Tchaikovsky Competition.

Van Cliburn was winner that year.

Second prize was awarded to a slender, six-foot-one, nineteen-year-old Chinese pianist named Liu Shih-kun.

Van Cliburn gained immediate worldwide recognition. Liu Shih-kun returned to China, forgotten by the Western world.

What eventually happened to the young Chinese pianist is almost too terrible to imagine. Yet it happened. And the lost years of Liu Shih-kun comprise THE REST OF THE STORY.

After Chinese pianist Liu Shih-kun earned second prize in the Tchaikovsky Competition, he returned to his homeland.

By the mid-1960s he was an established concert artist in China. But trouble was brewing—a so-called Cultural Revolution headed by Madame Chiang Ching, the wife of Mao Tse-tung.

A purge is what it was. Anything and everything of Western influence had fallen into disfavor.

Western music was also a victim of this revolutionary wrath, and so pianist Liu Shih-kun, for refusing to renounce the music he had loved since childhood, was deemed "an enemy of the people" and imprisoned.

Locked away where no one could see, he was beaten mercilessly. From the assault, a bone in his right forearm was cracked.

For the next six years, pianist Liu Shih-kun languished in a tiny prison cell. There was no book to read, save the teachings of Mao, no paper on which to write, and most significantly of all—there was no piano.

For six long years.

Very possibly he would be there still, had Richard Nixon not built an East-West bridge across the Pacific Ocean and opened his prison door. In the new spirit of mutual respect an imprisoned concert pianist would have been an embarrassment to the People's Republic.

For the purpose of propaganda, Liu was released from jail and requested to perform in Peking with the Philadelphia Orchestra. The request was from Madame Chiang Ching, the woman who had ordered his abuse and incarceration in the first place.

Could the propagandists have been so naïve as to imagine a pianist could perform after six years without a piano, or did they suspect what you are about to learn?

For indeed, upon his release, pianist Liu Shih-kun performed with the Philadelphia Orchestra in Peking. And extraordinarily well!

After a subsequent eighteen months in prison, bringing his accumulated time of incarceration to seven and a half years, he was released once more—and again he played brilliantly!

Liu Shih-kun never returned to prison after that. Although he remained the same, the political and cultural climate of his country had changed. He is at last accepted at home, at last emerging into the international limelight denied him for twenty-one years.

That he has survived is remarkable itself. That his *hands* have survived, as though they had never stopped playing, is being called by musicians everywhere "astounding."

For when they locked Liu up more than a decade ago, the cultural revolutionaries stripped him of everything musical. Any of his possessions that had anything to do with music were destroyed. Even a lock of Franz Liszt's hair, won in a piano competition when Liu was sixteen, was burned.

In prison he was denied a piano, denied even paper which might be used to recapture the music he had lost.

Yet an invaluable something was left Liu Shih-kun, something which in turn produced notes of music and produced a piano keyboard in his lonely prison cell. That of which the Red Guards could not deprive the artist.

For seven and a half years in a tiny prison cell, Liu Shih-kun practiced his beloved music in his vivid, disciplined imagination—on a piano no one else could see!

11. Search Me— I Dare You

In the July 19, 1948, edition of *Time* magazine, under the heading of "National Affairs," under the subheading of "Heros"—a heroine.

A young woman newly awarded the Medal of Freedom. A lady they called Joey.

Joey was, in fact, Mrs. Josefina Guerrero from Manila, a society figure in her native country.

During World War II, Joey was a spy. Our side. And she was the best. For all the secret maps and messages she carried back and forth across enemy lines, she was never apprehended, never searched once.

How Joey was able to achieve her remarkable wartime record is THE REST OF THE STORY.

Josefina Guerrero was the toast of Manila.

She was young, pretty, vivacious; her husband was a wealthy medical student at Santo Tomás University. Everything was going her way.

That was before the war.

After the Japanese invaded the Philippines, Josefina joined her friends—the other young matrons of Manila— and together they worked to help the internees and the U.S. prisoners of war, bringing them food, clothing, medicine, messages.

When the Americans landed on Leyte, Josefina offered to become a spy.

She had already gained valuable experience in the Manilan underground; she would be the best spy the Americans ever had, she said. And we, smiling at her youthful enthusiasm, agreed.

On her first mission, she mapped the waterfront fortifications of the Japanese and the locations of enemy anti-aircraft batteries. Armed with nothing more than a sketchbook and a pencil, she prowled the restricted areas, recording all that she saw.

From Josefina's drawings, American planes were able to pinpoint their targets.

The success of this and of subsequent missions earned Josefina the respect of her allies and it brought her an affectionate nickname, Joey.

Joey, it seemed, could do no wrong in the pursuit of espionage. Because of her conspicuous bravery, many near-impossible tasks were accomplished in the line of duty.

One mission took her through fifty-six miles of Japanese encampments and checkpoints and freshly sown minefields. With a top-secret map taped to her back, she trudged those fifty-six miles on foot.

For three years, Joey continued her cloak-and-dagger career. Then one day the war was over, and with it ended Joey's job as a spy.

A grateful U.S. War Department awarded her the Medal of Freedom with silver palm for having saved "untold" American lives. Visiting the United States, Joey was presented with a Catholic medallion by Francis Cardinal Spellman for her "valorous and heroic actions."

But if there was one testimony to her ultimate success in espionage, it was that she lived to tell about it. Joey—Josefina Guerrero—was never caught. Stopped many times by suspicious Japanese, she was never apprehended, never even searched.

For Joey had a secret weapon, an unconditional insurance policy to which any other spy would be unlikely to subscribe. An impenetrable barrier, if you will.

Her unfailing deterrent to those who would detain her was an authentic disease . . . called leprosy!

12. Nice Try

Let's say you're thirteen years old, born and reared in another country, and you're looking for a fast ten dollars.

Would it ever occur to you to write a letter—simply requesting ten Yankee dollars—to the President of the United States?

It did occur to one thirteen-year-old.

In fact, the audacity of that letter was so striking that it is retained to this day in our National Archives. The year was 1940 and the rest is THE REST OF THE STORY.

In the autumn of 1940 he was a boy of thirteen, receiving a strict private parochial school education.

Now certainly every youngster of that age wants attention. This one wanted prestige. Daily he pondered his anonymity and a way to be rid of it—a way to become a big shot with his classmates.

Then it came to him.

In school he had learned a great deal about the United States of America, the wealthiest and most powerful and most generous nation in the entire world. What if he could somehow con the President of the United States out of ten dollars?

The idea became an obsession.

He would have to write a letter of some kind, carefully worded of course, a letter requesting the money while dangling a vague promise of something in return.

The youngster had studied just enough English to get his subtle point across in writing.

He addressed the letter to President Franklin Roosevelt, asking outright for ten dollars because ". . . I have not seen a ten dollars bill green american and I would like to have one of them. . . ."

He went on to hint, almost in postscript, that his country

41

was rich in iron ore—and *he* knew where the President could get his hands on some!

Next day, the letter was in the mail. Proudly its young author announced to his friends that President Roosevelt was going to send him some money.

His friends laughed. Surely he didn't expect an answer from the President, much less a handout.

The scoffing of the youngsters shook him awake. What if President Roosevelt just tossed the letter into the wastebasket? He had boasted prematurely and now he might have to pay for it in ridicule.

But the little fellow did receive an answer. The response was written by an embassy counselor on behalf of the President of the United States:

"The President has directed the embassy to acknowledge, with an expression of appreciation, your letter of November 6, 1940, written on the occasion of his reelection."

No ten dollars.

Nice try.

But when the boy brought that letter of recognition to school, the Roman Catholic sisters were sufficiently impressed to put it on the school bulletin board for a whole week.

They didn't know their little lad had tried to hit FDR for a fast ten.

Neither could they have guessed that the U.S. State Department would save the youngster's letter, only to review it with amazement thirty-eight years later.

For the thirteen-year-old boy who wished only to be important in the eyes of his classmates became important in revolution.

You know him.

Fidel Castro.

13. The Death of John Dillinger

John Dillinger. Public Enemy Number One.

There is still a great deal of controversy over how and when he died. Now, at last, let's set the record straight.

In May of 1934, John Dillinger was hiding out. He had heard that many prominent gangland figures were submitting to plastic surgery, were having their faces changed and their fingerprints obliterated in order to become less recognizable, less detectable. The prospect fascinated Dillinger.

He called his lawyer and the lawyer mentioned the name of a German-born surgeon—a Dr. Loeser.

Loeser had practiced in Chicago for nearly thirty years. He had done time in Leavenworth on a narcotics rap; now he was out, in need of cash.

But was he good, Dillinger wanted to know? Yes, Loeser was a magician with a knife.

So the arrangements were made, and on the evening of May 27, 1934, John Dillinger arrived at a weatherbeaten two-story shack on Chicago's North Side. If all went well, Public Enemy Number One would emerge incognito, surgically, permanently.

Dillinger's lawyer met him at the house, explained the details.

The place was owned by a former speakeasy operator. No problem there. Dr. Loeser and his assistant would arrive the next day. The flat fee was five grand, one third to the lawyer. The operation would take place in a bedroom and Dillinger would recuperate in a back room.

Dillinger nodded, satisfied that everything was running smoothly.

In the morning, the doctor and his young assistant were brought to the house.

Dr. Loeser was apparently confident. The assistant, on the other hand, appeared pale, nervous, dissipated.

Loeser examined Dillinger's heart, asked if he wanted a local or a general anesthetic. Dillinger asked for a general.

Specifically, surgically, what was it that Dillinger wanted done?

The badman explained that he wanted three moles and a scar removed; he wanted a depression on the bridge of his nose filled and the dimple on his chin erased. Oh, yes . . . and the fingerprints. They must come off too.

Loeser agreed. Dillinger disrobed, lay down on a cot. It was expected that in a matter of hours, the familiar face on the Post Office wall would be no more.

Loeser went into the bathroom to wash his hands. Dillinger rested patiently as the assistant fashioned a mask out of toweling. Through this, the ether would be administered. The gangster began to draw deep breaths.

But in his nervousness, the young asistant gave too much ether too quickly. Dillinger's face was turning blue.

The assistant started shouting. Dr. Loeser hurried from the bathroom. Dillinger had swallowed his tongue.

Loeser grabbed a forceps, removed the gangster's tongue from his throat. There was still no breathing.

John Dillinger—Public Enemy Number One—was dead.

In a run-down shack on Chicago's North Side, just prior to cosmetic surgery, John Dillinger died. An overdose of ether.

But the surgeon, Dr. Loeser, would not give up. He abruptly began artificial respiration. Eventually Dillinger, who had technically expired, revived.

It was twenty-five days later, after successful surgery,

that John Dillinger strode from a Chicago theater with the "Lady in Red" . . . and the FBI shot him dead.

That's what history has said.

But you know THE REST OF THE STORY. You know John Dillinger died twice.

14. The Artistic Type

"I know what art is—it's the development of a man. An artist is not producing things, he's evolving himself."

John said that.

John is an artist, a romantic, a classically sensitive man.

Few serious artists in this age could hope for John's success. His smallest lithographs sell for no less than two-hundred dollars apiece; his watercolors bring between a thousand and fifteen hundred dollars; his oil paintings have sold for six thousand dollars.

Not long ago, a shopping-center art gallery sold sixty-four thousand dollars' worth a month.

John's art is represented in forty museums throughout the world.

New York's Metropolitan Museum of Art holds five of his paintings.

"Painting is like being in love for the first time." John said that.

So it should not surprise you to learn that despite his financial success, he continues to be motivated by an intangible ideal. He would, in fact, continue to paint for the same reason he began: he cannot live without it.

Even though you know this artist well, perhaps you never really knew him as you will when you learn THE REST OF THE STORY.

An artist is all he ever really wanted to be. In grammar school he won a contest sponsored by the American Society for the Prevention of Cruelty to Animals. For his drawing of a sad and bedraggled little dog he received the Humanitus award.

Upon graduating from high school, he received a second award for his art: the St. Gaudens Plaque. The New York City school system offers only one each year.

As a sophomore fine arts major at New York University,

John organized his own art school in Greenwich Village, the Village Academy of Art at 129 MacDougal Street. In two years—while John was still a senior in college—several of his works were accepted by the Metropolitan Museum of Art for its permanent collection.

In the years since, John's paintings have appeared in dozens of prestigious private collections also, including those of mayors, governors, senators, congressmen, respected church officials and international celebrities. The collection of Field Marshal Montgomery holds one of John's paintings.

Recently asked about plans for the future, John said: "Most of all I want to spend more time with my sweet Marie, the wife of my youth who abides with me still."

John is fond of Sean O'Casey's line "Let us find ways to spin joy into every moment of tomorrow's day."

Those words are so like John, the eternal romantic, the internationally revered and successful artist whose sensitivity as such is mostly hidden from the rest of the world.

For though John would rather you remember him as an artist, he has another job—another role in life that might suggest he is anything but sensitive.

The boy whose artistic career was launched with a drawing of a lonely puppy, the mature artist whose secret life is wrapped in canvas and colors and dreams, is also "Steve McGarrett," the hard-hitting uncompromising Irish cop of television's "Hawaii Five-O."

John's friends call him Jack. Jack Lord.

15. The Deciding Vote

Stephen Van Rensselaer took his job seriously.

Already in his sixties, Van Rensselaer had spent more than half his life in politics. Now, for the past three years, he had faithfully served the state of New York as representative in Congress.

Having seen a good deal of action on the floor of the House of Representatives, Van Rensselaer had become accustomed to the stresses of his profession. The good judgment and immediacy of his decision could, on any given day, affect the whole country.

Van Rensselaer knew it, and he was not afraid of it.

But after all the months and years of voting on the issues, large and small, one day there arose an issue on which Van Rensselaer simply could not decide.

And wouldn't you know it?

His vote was to be the deciding one!

How Congressman Van Rensselaer finally made up his mind is THE REST OF THE STORY.

At the age of twenty-five, Stephen Van Rensselaer got his first taste of politics as a member of the New York state legislature.

In two years he would be elected to the state senate, and in four more years, to the post of lieutenant governor for one term.

Vitally interested in the project which would one day link the Hudson River to the Great Lakes by water, Van Rensselaer was among the earliest advocates of the Erie Canal.

For fifteen years he served on the state's canal commission, parrying a good number of thorny proposals.

After the canal operation was secure, he turned his attention to the development of a school at Troy, New York, a school which became the Rensselaer Polytechnic Institute.

Decision making had become a way of life for Stephen Van Rensselaer. Important decision making.

His earliest training in the military, coupled with thirty-six years of active politics, *should* have enabled him to make up his mind with the swiftness and certainty of the veteran planner he was.

And yet, after only three years in Congress, came the decision Stephen Van Rensselaer simply could not make.

The issue did not take him by surprise. It had in fact been open to discussion for quite some while.

During the earliest phase of its consideration, Van Rensselaer had placed himself firmly on one side. But as the arguments dragged on Van Rensselaer wore down, lost his initial confidence.

This time the fire-tempered, thoroughly adept decision maker was squarely on the fence—disconcerting enough, had fate not deemed Van Rensselaer's vote a tie breaker.

The House of Representatives was neatly, evenly divided on the issue. All awaited the final word, the deciding vote of Stephen Van Rensselaer.

The heat was on and the senior representative from New York was warm. On February 9, Van Rensselaer took his seat in the House. Still undecided, no authority to petition, nowhere to look . . . but up!

So Stephen looked up in the only way he knew how. He bowed his head low on the desk in front of him: O Lord, please! *Please* . . .

The "please" was sufficient. Stephen opened his eyes, and the first thing he saw was something on the floor: a trampled, discarded ballot, already filled out!

The congressman, taking his first sight out of prayer as providence, cast the ballot. The issue was decided once and for all; the House of Representatives had spoken.

But the tie broken in the House had itself broken a

larger tie, an evenly divided popular vote . . . in the presidential election of 1824.

So it was by one vote, by one discarded ballot on the floor of Congress—and a prayer—that John Quincy Adams became the sixth President of the United States!

16. Maid to Sing

This is the Deep South you never knew. A dimension of Dixie that makes headlines only indirectly.

In Laurel, Mississippi, the Chisholms have always been a leading family. Forty years ago it was no less true; Mr. and Mrs. Alexander Chisholm were the epitome of their social community.

The Chisholms' housekeeper, Everlina, had been with them for forty-five years and the relationship between employee and employers was much more than that.

That was nearly a quarter of a century prior to the Civil Rights Act of 1957, when brotherhood was not yet enforceable by law. So when Everlina's little niece came over to play with the Chisholm daughters, it was not an avantgarde concession on behalf of the prestigious Chisholms. It came naturally.

And when Everlina's niece expressed the desire to become a grand lady someday, it was Mrs. Chisholm who willingly took the tiny black girl under her wing. She gently guided her in etiquette and in apparel and prepared her as best she could to face the world with pride.

Before such concern became fashionable, Mrs. Chisholm was the child's second mother, a concerned parent for whom the boundaries of color were no boundaries at all.

During school vacations, the young girl asked if she could help her aunt Everlina around the house.

Mrs. Chisholm and Everlina, eager to have her nearby, agreed. The girl went to work for ten dollars a week.

As the housekeeper's young niece worked about the Chisholm home, she sang. The young girl sang so well, in fact, that one day Mrs. Chisholm was inspired to call the child to the piano.

Within minutes, Mrs. Chisholm—a trained musician her-

51

self—was able to detect a rare, natural musical gift. The girl's tonal memory was excellent, her sense of pitch, precise.

How would she like to become a singer? Mrs. Chisholm asked.

A little chill went up the girl's spine. Her most prized possessions were recordings of Marian Anderson and other opera stars. Whenever the Metropolitan broadcast its productions, she would hasten to the radio and listen, spellbound.

Yes, the young girl assured Mrs. Chisholm, she would like very much to become a singer. From that day on, each step was one step closer to the realization of her dream.

At subsequent gatherings in the Chisholm home, Mrs. Chisholm happily amazed her guests by presenting the slender young girl in a maid's uniform who could sing the classics with virtuosity and sensitivity beyond her years.

When in time the girl was old enough, it was Mrs. Chisholm who sponsored her education and sent her to the Juilliard School in New York to study voice.

Today, many years and a succession of successes later, she and the Chisholm family are still family, are still close, and surely always will be.

And the phenomenal operatic talent, the long-reigning empress of the Metropolitan Opera stage, the girl who once worked as a maid in Laurel, Mississippi—and whom love sent out into the world—is Leontyne Price.

And now you know THE REST OF THE STORY.

17. The "Gay" Duke of Orleans

Anne was a devoted mother, deeply concerned about her son's effeminacy. Her greatest worry was that he, her son, was not effeminate enough!

Anne was rearing her little boy as a little girl—and for what she believed was a very good reason. Her reason is THE REST OF THE STORY.

Anne sometimes referred to her boy child as "my little girl." His name was Philippe.

Through most of his childhood he wore petticoats. He was instilled with a love for trinkets, jewelry, lace, ribbons.

Few young ladies in all of history have been instructed as conscientiously to that end as was Philippe.

Yet there was a method in what must appear his mother's madness. For Anne had an older son whose name was Louis. King Louis XIV of France. In an era when the rivalry of brothers for a throne was not uncommon, Anne would see to it that the younger Philippe was reared to the contrary of all such ambition.

Louis was to be king, and that was that.

Louis's brother Philippe, the Duke of Orleans, seduced into a narcissistic haze, guided in the ways of effete submissiveness since his birth, would by this design pose no threat to his elder brother's throne.

His delicate, effeminate behavior amused the royal court. The closest he ever came to conflict with the King were those arguments in which he was described as "a Pomeranian yapping at a lion."

In battle he was praised for his "most feminine martial courage," though he was usually late to the fray—as a duchess might be tardy for the Grand Ball. He arrived at the lines painted, powdered, covered with ribbons and diamonds, his long eyelashes batting in the breeze. He never wore a hat to battle for fear of flattening his wig. Rather than death, he feared what the sun and dust might do to his complexion.

Philippe quickly grew weary of warfare, preferring the click of his high heels in marble halls to gunpowder and flying musketballs. The pomp and perfume of the royal court were his cup of tea, and all his life it would be.

This much may be said: His mother had succeeded in her purpose.

Philippe, Duke of Orleans, enemy to physical exercise and champion of idle chatter, was never to challenge Louis's authority as King, nor even to comprehend the meaning of politics.

A sissy Mother wanted, a sissy she got—in spades.

There is a prevalent question today involving the definition of "gay": Is a homosexual born or made? This next does not answer that riddle. But it comes close. For Philippe, Duke of Orleans, influenced in every conceivable way to become a "young lady," should at least have become exclusively "gay."

Instead, he had a mistress.

And two wives.

And eleven legitimate children.

No historian will dare speculate as to how many illegitimate ones.

Thus Philippe, the King's brother who might have been a "queen," is remembered instead as the "grandfather of Europe."

Every subsequent Roman Catholic royal family lists him among its ancestors.

All the kings of France after his brother Louis, as well as Marie Antoinette—and the son of Napoleon—were descended from him!

18. Going to Hell
with Dr. Morell

Dr. Theodor Morell. What he lacks in competence is compensated for by charisma. He is introduced to prospective patients socially, makes an impression, and the impressionable are hooked—eventually, in every sense of the term.

A specific case for your consideration . . .

Dr. Morell is invited to a private home. His host complains of intestinal trouble.

The doctor appears concerned; how long has the discomfort been going on?

Intermittently for quite some time.

Nodding pensively and without hesitation, Dr. Morell offers his diagnosis and his suggested treatment.

Later the patient remarks: "Nobody has ever before told me so clearly and precisely what is wrong with me. His method of cure is so logical that I have the greatest confidence in him. I shall follow his prescriptions to the letter."

These "logical" prescriptions include exotic bacteria and hormones and phosphorus and dextrose and belladonna . . . and strychnine. Not enough strychnine to kill the patient, of course. The dangerous if not entirely evil Dr. Morell requires the dependence of his patient, for money, for prestige . . . and for his sinister experimentation.

After a few weeks the patient notices an improvement in his condition. His own words are: "What luck that I met Morell! He has saved my life. Wonderful, the way he has helped me!"

In time the patient's sense of well-being will be heightened beyond his dreams. For Dr. Morell will add to his prescriptive arsenal—amphetamines. Speed.

By Morell's own admission his patient "was really never

sick." Not before he was introduced to Dr. Morell, anyway. Now it's a different story.

Now the slightest complaint is answered by pills and injections, a variety of medications spanning the questionable to the occult. And the result is a shuffling, stumbling, trembling, emaciated, glassy-eyed, gray-complexioned shell of a man. A human wreck.

Submerged in a sea of uppers and downers, he sleeps no more than three hours a night. Uneasy sleep.

In months he appears to age years.

And *still* he professes his confidence in Dr. Morell.

Truth is—he needs the speed . . .

In this specific case the "treatments" lasted nine years, astounding considering the quantities of atropine and strychnine and amphetamines consumed by the patient in that period of time.

Twenty-eight types of drugs in all, their direct and side effects compounded. The speed took the highest toll.

We shall neither forget nor forgive Dr. Morell's patient, the man he was in the beginning, the monster he became. Yet the monumental irony of his association with a megalomaniac physician was that in the end, the master mesmerist was mesmerized, the predator became prey . . .

The name of Dr. Theodor Morell has dropped into obscurity.

Remembered instead is his patient, a speed freak who spent the last decade of his life shattered and shaking and with his brains in a basket, the man who on earth went to hell—because of Dr. Morell.

Hitler was "high."

And now you know THE REST OF THE STORY.

19. Talk of the Town

Her name was Pauline.

And she was the talk of the town.

As the nineteenth century blossomed in Paris, so did she. For Pauline, the style to which she had become accustomed was the very essence of *joie de vivre*.

Her upper-crust critics in Paris society put it another way: Pauline had no morals.

Yet about each old lover she discarded and each new lover she entangled in her web, the pre-jet set of beautiful young people delighted and gossiped, tacitly begging for news of her newest adventure.

Perhaps Pauline's activities were not all that rare for a young lady of nineteenth-century France. But because she was a member of the royal court, her whereabouts and whatabouts were of great interest and were widely observed.

Her *who*abouts were most shocking of all.

By the age of sixteen, Pauline had taken on the high-echelon military. That is, she had had affairs with most of the French Army's general staff.

To the relief of the generals' wives Pauline then concentrated her affections on one unmarried general, an upstanding officer named Victor Emmanuel Leclerc.

Pauline and Leclerc were married. What Pauline did not know was that Leclerc's new assignment was far from the tapestry and tinsel of Paris, was thousands of miles away in Haiti, the Caribbean colony of Saint Domingue.

It took six soldiers, including husband Leclerc, to cart the protesting Pauline aboard ship.

Upon their arrival, however, Pauline adapted to her new

surroundings as though she had never left Paris.

When Leclerc took his twenty-five thousand troops out into the Haitian jungle to deal with the rebels, Pauline remained in the capital city, Port-au-Prince.

Entertaining her husband's leftover soldiers, Pauline threw extravagant parties and began a ritual for which she soon became famous: daily milk baths.

Pauline rarely bathed alone, which accounted for the healthy complexions of the French officers serving in Saint Domingue.

Victor Leclerc clearly got the short end of this overseas assignment. Within a short while, he contracted yellow fever and died. Shedding a brief crocodile tear, the general's wife caught the next eastbound ship.

Soon she was back in her beloved Paris, returning to the serious business of making scandal.

Years of milk-bathing and scores of lovers followed.

There was even another marriage—this time to an Italian prince who heaped upon Pauline a fortune in jewels and a wardrobe of six hundred gowns. Predictably, her favorite gown—was transparent.

At forty, Pauline took to fretting over wrinkles; five years later, she was dead. The gossips of Paris had lost their most tantalizing subject.

For Pauline, the red-hot mama of the pre-jet jet set, the talk of nineteenth-century Paris, the young woman who took bathing beyond the realm of good clean fun—was more than just a high-born lady with a weakness for men in uniform.

She was the sister . . . of Napoleon Bonaparte.

Now you know THE REST OF THE STORY.

20. The Body
Behind the Voice

He was the fastest rising young singing star in San Francisco. He was called the "Romantic Voice of America." Teen-age girls from the bay to the hills would have given about anything—just for a glimpse of him.

Yet none of his adoring fans had ever seen him.

Not so much as a photograph!

The reason behind this incredible incognito is THE REST OF THE STORY.

When he was four years old, there seemed no doubt he would become a fine pianist one day. A concert pianist. That had been the thrust of his childhood—long hours of practice, accumulation of repertoire.

In his teens came a dose of realism. The musicians who were eating regularly were the commercial talents, the popular players. So the young man reluctantly switched to popular music and applied for a job as staff musician at radio station KFRC in San Francisco.

The station manager acknowledged the affable eighteen-year-old's considerable keyboard prowess. Unfortunately, they already had a piano player. What the station needed was a singer.

"Ever do any singing?" the manager asked.

The young man glanced downward, mentioned something about a church choir. He had been a boy soprano.

"Let's hear you sing, then!"

The young man sang.

It was a pleasant voice indeed! Tenor range, pitch perfect, rather dreamy.

He would start work on Monday. Monday came and went, and before long KFRC was receiving some very enthusiastic fan mail for their new balladeer.

The station became equally enthusiastic, began billing their young tenor as the "Romantic Voice of America."

The fan mail persisted, augmented. Teen-age girls in the listening audience fell in love with the voice, begged for signed photographs.

No photos would be sent. And the young crooner knew why. It would be just too embarrassing for him, too disillusioning for his fans.

For the same reason, public appearances were out of the question. The romantic, golden voice would remain a prisoner of the airwaves.

And then one day, a young lady admirer—overcome by her crush and her curiosity—ventured into the corridors of KFRC in search of her singing idol.

Unknowingly, it was *he* whom she met in the hall, and of whom she asked directions.

Blushing, he mumbled something and was about to turn away when a station secretary, unaware of his predicament, leaned out of a doorway and called his name.

Stunned by the revelation, the young lady fan flashed a blank expression—and then she began to laugh. Hilariously. Uncontrollably. The "Romantic Voice of America" was a five-foot-ten teen-ager—who weighed two hundred and sixty pounds!

Even after her laughter had subsided, it rang painfully in the young man's ears.

Then and there he decided to lose the weight that was restricting his career. He would emerge from the Fat Closet to match the romantic image of his voice. He would be proud to be seen and, one grueling four-month diet later, he was.

Television viewers know him from the Late Show as a trim and handsome young actor—and from his own show, wherein he has been critically acknowledged as "the total performer."

Yet once upon a time, thirty-six years and sixty pounds ago, there was an eighteen-year-old overweight golden-voiced crooner who might have hidden behind a microphone all his life—and was instead embarrassed to stardom.

You know him as Merv Griffin.

21. The Pad

Clotworthy Skeffington, the Second Earl of Massereene, in 1765 at the age of twenty-three, visited Paris. He liked it so much he stayed for twenty-four years.

Perhaps so would you have stayed, had you found the circumstances of elegance and grace enjoyed by the Earl of Massereene.

What *was* the life he loved?

The Earl of Massereene was so comfortable in Paris and in his surroundings that in twenty years he left his suite of apartments only once or twice.

And if you think this is carrying Home Sweet Home a bit too far, try to understand it from the Earl's viewpoint.

The outdoors offered little allure. There was hunting, perhaps, but hunting was a comparatively dreary sport, remarkably uncivilized.

Everything that the Earl really enjoyed could be enjoyed in the sanctity of his apartment: parties, card games, dancing, fencing, books, music, friends.

So, in 1769, the Earl simply closed the door on the outside world and retired to a life of sublime confinement.

Among the first demands placed on his staff was to collect a stock of the finest wines. Those wines must be of the proper age, the Earl warned his steward, neither too seasoned nor too fresh. The steward set about his task.

Next, the Earl began to collect books. His library would one day be the most outstanding in Paris, he told his friends. If in the end it was not, it certainly came close.

The Earl's first party in his new suite of apartments must have been sumptuous. The best French chefs prepared the food. The best known of Paris society attended. There was even an orchestra to serenade, and later to accompany dancing.

For the Earl of Massereene, twenty years of personal tradition was only beginning.

The Earl also quickly learned that one was not required to leave his dwelling to be a playboy. The most beautiful women in the city came to *him*.

On these lovely ladies the Earl heaped all imaginable gifts. Precious jewels and huge wardrobes of the most exquisite clothing.

After a few years, this life of bachelorhood wore thin. The Earl met Marie Anne Barcier, a woman of legendary beauty, and he married her. And they continued to live a life of frivolous festivity and extraordinary comfort. All . . . in the Earl's apartment.

But all things change. In July of 1789 revolution brought an end to the Earl of Massereene's pampered existence.

Against a counterpoint of musket fire and clattering swords he fled, at last, his suite of sumptuous apartments, his fine wines, his select library, the good times. Reluctantly, he returned to Ireland.

Historians tell us that history repeats itself—that civilization, though continuous, reflects the past.

But when else in history could the luxurious life of the Earl of Massereene have been lived?

At what other time could a man retreat to a glorious suite of apartments for twenty years without emerging and continue to receive the income from his estate—while keeping his creditors at bay?

For Clotworthy Skeffington, the Second Earl of Massereene, for twenty years reveled in the existence of which you've just read . . . in debtor's prison.

And now you know THE REST OF THE STORY.

22. All in His Mind

Benjamin Banneker was a distinguished black scholar.

Born in Ellicott, Maryland, he attended private school there. Later he established his reputation as a mathematician and astronomer with an unsurpassed knowledge of technical diagramming and data.

It came as a surprise to no one when Benjamin Banneker was appointed by the U.S. Secretary of State to a select engineering team of six men who would lay the groundwork for a modern city.

Today three quarters of a million people live in that city, entirely unaware of the fact that at one time every building and byway had been lost . . . and found.

It was a logical choice, that of renowned scientist and scholar Benjamin Banneker, to join the engineering team which would prepare to build a modern city.

The internationally respected group of masterminds was to be headed by French architect Charles L'Enfant. His plan was to be used.

An elaborate plan it was! Filled with futuristic architecture and grand parkways and streets designed to accommodate both beautiful vistas and rapid transit, it was to be a city of contemporary elegance and of communication.

Unfortunately for architect L'Enfant, he soon found himself in the midst of a political scandal. Land speculators wanted to know the prime locations and exact boundaries of the new city. L'Enfant refused to divulge them until they had become a matter of public record. The city commissioners then accused the architect of attempting to control the distribution of land for his own purposes, and eventually L'Enfant was dismissed on superficially unrelated grounds.

Thus before the land itself had been completely surveyed,

the chief engineer and sole architect had returned to Paris *with* his plans.

With the chief engineer gone, the plans for the city gone, the Secretary of State called an emergency meeting of the commissioners, surveyors and engineers. Among them was mathematician Benjamin Banneker.

The discouraged Secretary briefly summed up the situation, advised those assembled that a new plan, a brand-new city design, would have to be drawn. Were there any suggestions?

Benjamin Banneker stood, and every eye turned to him as he asked if the *old* plans had been satisfactory.

What difference did that make? everyone wanted to know. The ream of intricate architecture was on its way back to France, under the arm of the original architect!

But Benjamin assured them that he had studied the maps and the plans as they had come from L'Enfant's drawing board and he, Benjamin, was quite certain that he remembered every detail.

The committee's initial reaction to Banneker's bold claim was disbelief that anyone could completely recall the myriad complexities of an entire city! To memorize the architectural details of a solitary building would have been phenomenal enough.

If anyone's brain was equal to the task, Benjamin Banneker's was.

Shortly thereafter, the original plans were precisely reproduced. In time a magnificent city arose—from a memory.

You may have visited that city. You might live there. For once upon a time, a man named Benjamin Banneker strode streets of paper—all in his mind—and today those streets are real.

We may not remember Ben as the publisher of an internationally respected almanac, or as the maker of the first American-made clock.

But now we can never forget Benjamin Banneker, the man whose remarkable memory was trusted by Secretary of State Thomas Jefferson. For the plans Banneker had carried in his mind were those of Washington, D.C.

And now you know THE REST OF THE STORY.

23. Androcles Revisited

A century ago, not quite forty miles from the city of Paris, was the Forest of Fontainebleau. That resplendent woodland was a Mecca for young artists in search of subject matter, a magical place of pure inspiration where friendly deer nuzzled passersby and undisturbed foliage grew up in grand design. There, as nowhere else on earth, playful lights and shadows teased the eye.

Among the enthralled artistic pilgrims was an aspiring painter in his early twenties, Pierre.

Many times Pierre made the two-day walk from Paris to the Forest of Fontainebleau just to set up his easel and canvas in the quiet.

One day the woods were more quiet than usual.

The birds were silent; the deer did not come as so often before to beg a crust of bread or to watch Pierre's brush in ballet.

Soon Pierre learned why: There was a stranger in the glade, a dazed, ragged, mud-spattered stranger stumbling through the tall grass as though he had been pursued by the devil himself.

A desperate voice called to Pierre, shattering the stillness. "Please help me!" it said. "I am dying of hunger!"

The intruder fairly collapsed at the young artist's feet. Between gulps of water and bread his story unfolded.

His name was Raoul Rigaud.

He was a journalist who had opposed in print France's authoritarian government, and now he was being hunted by the imperial authorities.

It had been a narrow escape.

They had surprised him at his apartment; he had made it out a window and to the balcony of an apartment adjoining his. Through that window and down a flight of stairs and into the street and onto a departing train. It had all happened so fast!

Next thing he knew Raoul was wandering aimlessly through a dense forest, the Forest of Fontainebleau. That was days ago. Now he was exhausted, starving. He would give himself up.

Pierre listened sympathetically.

No, declared the young artist, Raoul would not surrender to the authorities! He would stay right there in the woods and wait while Pierre fetched a disguise. There was a village nearby. Pierre would find an artist's smock and a painting kit, and before sundown Raoul Rigaud would be just another artist visitor to the Forest of Fontainebleau.

Raoul remained at Pierre's side for several weeks until the journalist's friends in Paris could be notified. The friends then made arrangements for Raoul to flee France safely.

The parting of Pierre and Raoul was bittersweet. Tears of gratitude filled the fugitive's eyes as he shook Pierre's hand for the last time.

"Had it not been for you . . ." he started to say.

Then he turned, and was gone.

A number of years passed.

Now it was the spring of 1871.

Only weeks before, Napoleon III had been officially deposed; the revolutionary Commune had seized power in Paris.

Pierre, just thirty, was in Paris too.

He was painting on the banks of the Seine one day when some national guardsmen stopped to look at his work. The Communard soldiers were quiet at first, but as Pierre continued to paint he heard them muttering to each other.

Suddenly one of the soldiers snatched Pierre's unfinished canvas from its easel. Pierre was fooling no one, the guardsman said; Pierre was a spy for the Versailles forces and this so-called painting was proof!

But it *was* a painting, Pierre protested. What possible threat could a mere painting pose to the Paris Commune?

The soldier's gaze was stern. "What do you see here?" he asked his comrades, thrusting Pierre's canvas before them. "A picture, yes—but a picture of what?"

Another guardsman spoke up: obviously it was a secret plan, a diagram of the Seine area showing vulnerable points and strategic locations to guide the Versailles troops.

"An aid to the enemy!" shouted another.

By now a small crowd had gathered on the river bank. Who was this Pierre? they wanted to know. A spy for Versailles? Then throw him in the Seine! Drown him!

But Communard "law" provided for a more orderly disposal of spies. The soldiers placed Pierre under arrest, led him off down the street toward the town hall of the Sixth Arrondissement. There a firing squad was on permanent duty to handle such matters.

The angry crowd followed, crying out for Pierre's death. Within a hundred steps their numbers had increased to mob proportions.

"Kill him!" they shouted in terrifying cadence. "Kill him!"

At the vortex of this human maelstrom was poor Pierre. He was not a spy. He was but a young artist trying to make his way in life—and soon, it seemed, his way was to end.

At the town hall Pierre's trial and conviction proved little more than a nod from the captain in charge. Down in the square the firing squad waited, the mob chanted.

As Pierre was being led, his hands bound behind him, to the place where he was to die, he returned in his mind to the Forest of Fontainebleau. He patted the grazing deer and watched the sunlight dance on the morning dew. If this world were to pass, perhaps the next would be more like that one in his secret heart.

But when Pierre opened his eyes it was not to see a line of raised rifles. It was to see the Communard Public Prosecutor pushing his way through the crowd. He was a grand sight indeed, dressed in full uniform with tricolor sash, and the soldiers in his attendance were equally magnificent.

Moments later the Public Prosecutor and Pierre were standing face to face. "Surely you remember me!" said the Prosecutor, and he embraced the young artist.

For the high Communard official who had just happened to be passing the square was none other than Raoul Rigaud, the onetime political fugitive whom Pierre had rescued in the Forest of Fountainebleau.

The attitude of the onlookers inverted at the sight of Raoul's embrace, and a great cheer came forth from the crowd.

Raoul demanded Pierre's release, after which he escorted the young artist to the town hall balcony overlooking the square. "Let us sing the 'Marseillaise' for our comrade!" cried Raoul.

And the people sang.

Pierre was given a pass to travel and to paint wherever he wished, and as his adventure drew to a close, life began anew.

Once upon a time, according to legend, there was a Roman slave named Androcles who pulled a thorn from a lion's paw. Later sentenced to death, Androcles met that same lion in the arena. Out of gratitude the hungry beast refused to devour Androcles, and the slave's much-impressed captors set him free.

Pierre felt that his was a real-life reenactment of that ancient fiction.

For it was a moment of thoughtfulness, a good deed, which acted indirectly upon his destiny, which blossomed to bestow upon the whole world a genius that might otherwise have consigned itself to oblivion . . . the fathomless depths of shadow and light . . . the everlasting art of Pierre-Auguste Renoir.

Now you know THE REST OF THE STORY.

24. McKeeby's Portrait

Almost everyone in Cedar Rapids, Iowa, knew him. He was B. H. McKeeby, the town's leading dentist.

Dr. McKeeby was a modest, quiet, conservative man. Not at all the sort who would boast of himself or his accomplishments. So you can imagine why he was reticent at first when one of his patients—a young man called Gus—asked to paint Dr. McKeeby's portrait.

Gus was as much a friend as a patient. He had helped decorate Dr. McKeeby's office and his home. And because Gus's teeth had had no early care, he provided a long-standing professional challenge to Dr. McKeeby.

Thus was the symbiotic nature of their relationship. But a portrait! Dr. McKeeby wasn't too sure about that.

Why would Gus want to paint *him,* anyway?

Gus assured the doctor that his face was one of a kind. And those *hands,* Gus would say. So long and large and strong! Dr. McKeeby was, according to Gus, the ideal artistic subject.

And what did Gus have in mind for this portrait? the doctor wanted to know.

What Gus had in mind—is THE REST OF THE STORY.

When Gus confided the theme of his intended painting to Dr. McKeeby, the respectable dentist politely—flatly—refused to pose.

Gus observed that the doctor was responding out of shyness more than anything else, and if it would make Dr. McKeeby feel any better, Gus assured him he would be painted in such a way that no one would ever recognize him.

On that condition, and still not quite certain how such artistic camouflage was possible, Dr. McKeeby reluctantly agreed to sit for the portrait.

You've guessed the rest.

When the painting was finished everyone, including and especially Dr. McKeeby, recognized Dr. McKeeby.

His atypical pose, in uncharacteristic clothes, was insufficient to disguise Cedar Rapids' foremost dentist.

Not even the portrait's anomalous setting could distract from Doc McKeeby's unmistakable visage.

Gus just shrugged.

Somehow, he had thought his friend would remain publicly dissociated from the painting.

After all, you didn't know it was Dr. McKeeby. Until now.

For "Gus" was the artist's nickname. His sister called him that.

His sister also appears in the portrait with their family dentist.

And just as Gus had promised Dr. McKeeby, he had also promised his sister that she would not be recognized—that the atypical severity of her posed expression would belie her identity as well.

In 1930, the Art Institute of Chicago bought Gus's painting for three hundred dollars.

It hangs there still. And over these nearly fifty years, it has remained perhaps the best-known, the most culturally significant masterwork by an American artist.

Subsequently a vehicle for merciless satire—from prime-time comedy to cornflakes commercials—the portrait which appears to depict a stern, solemn-faced, side-by-side Iowa farm couple had somewhat a satirical origin itself.

For the real-life Iowa farmers of the 1930s intuitively sensed the incongruous characterizations, without realizing what you now know.

Gus—whom you remember as Grant Wood—simply

couldn't find any farmers whose faces pleased him.

So he selected his sister and his dentist, Dr. McKeeby, who had never before held a pitchfork in his life.

Their portrait is known as *American Gothic*.

25. Amazing!

It was not uncommon, in eighteenth-century England, for a boy to spend several uninspiring months in boarding school and then head out to sea.

That's how it happened for John. When John was eleven, his father—a master of a ship in the Mediterranean trade —took the boy on board.

This early training provided excellent groundwork for John's next major seafaring experience, impressment into the British Navy.

Yet what John had gained from his father's knowledge of sailing, he had lost in discipline. John was soon arrested for desertion, publicly flogged and demoted to common sailor.

Still in his teens, John received permission to sail on the H.M.S. *Harwich*, bound for the African coast. By now, the unsettled and impatient youth was emerging as the rotten apple in the barrel.

Mocking authority, he chose his friends unwisely and "sank to the depths of vice."

In Africa, John fell into the service of a slave dealer. Slave trade began to fascinate John as a lucrative livelihood, but before he knew it, he was put to work on the dealer's plantation laboring with the other slaves.

At twenty-one, John escaped. Hopping an outbound ship called the *Greyhound*, he presently returned to the depravity of his teens.

Associating with the lowest of crew members, John ridiculed the upright seamen in his company, ridiculed the ship's captain—even ridiculed a book he had found on board. A book entitled *The Imitation of Christ*. Clearly, he remembered joking about that book one bright afternoon.

That night the *Greyhound* sailed into a violent storm.

John awakened to discover his cabin half filled with sea-water. The ship's side had caved in and the *Greyhound* was going down. The *Greyhound* had sailed into high seas; her side collapsed in the turbulence.

Ordinarily such damage would send a ship to the bottom within a few minutes. In this case, the *Greyhound's* buoyant cargo bought a few hours of precious time.

After nine hours at the pumps, John overheard a desperate remark from one of the crew. They were all goners, he said.

And almost in answer, John—unwittingly and for the first time in his life—prayed. "If this will not do, the Lord have mercy on us!"

The record shows that the *Greyhound* did not go down.

Although one might have expected John's prayer of emergency to be quickly forgotten, it was remembered unto his death. Each year he observed the anniversary of that most significant incident with prayer and fasting. In a very real sense, he observed it throughout each remaining day of his life.

For John retired from the sea to become a minister. Also a writer of verse.

And the immortal words of a bad boy turned good, the distant reflection of an event long past, are celebrated to this day:

> Amazing grace! how sweet the sound,
> That saved a wretch like me!
> I once was lost, but now am found,
> Was blind, but now I see.

John was John Newton. And now you know THE REST OF THE STORY.

26. The Remarkable Miss Neef

Thomas van Beek is forty-three. He lives in Amsterdam, his native Netherlands.

A respected businessman, in 1961 Tom was a twenty-five-year-old executive still testing his wings in the business world. And he was in need of a private secretary.

After a long, discouraging procession of unpromising applicants, a bright, charming young lady came to Tom's office.

She was Miss Neef. Her references were impressive, her typing and shorthand were more than adequate. And beyond her obvious secretarial talent was the aura of personal stability Tom had been looking for.

Miss Neef was hired on the spot.

After her first week on the job, Tom was certain that he had found the one and only solid-gold Girl Friday; she was an executive's dream.

When she answered the phone, she projected polite authority. The quality of her voice alone let the caller know that he was in touch with an efficient operation.

When, in the course of business, Miss Neef was faced with those myriad minor emergencies, she was always calm and her solution to each problem was quick, direct.

Miss Neef was tireless.

At the end of a long day, when even her young employer was completely exhausted, Miss Neef was fresh, energetic, apparently as prepared to cope with her responsibilities as she had been before her traditionally brief lunch break.

The weeks became months and the months, years. During the seasons of heavy business, Miss Neef did the work of two. She was a one-woman miracle, a credit to her employer, a major contributor to his subsequent professional success.

Then came 1973, and the day Tom had secretly dreaded for the past twelve years.

It was not another job offer, Miss Neef assured Tom, nor was it a matter of money. She had been quite happy in her career, but now she simply wished to retire as Tom's private secretary.

Businessman Thomas van Beek would miss his secretary of twelve years, but it was not his decision. He would accept Miss Neef's retirement as gracefully as possible.

As he thought about the splendid job she had done during those past twelve years—really more than anyone could have asked of one person—Tom was determined that his remarkable Miss Neef should have an appropriately generous retirement party.

It was on the occasion of that celebration that Tom learned THE REST OF THE STORY.

For shortly after the guest of honor had arrived—the guest of honor arrived. And the mystery of Miss Neef's boundless energy was not a mystery anymore.

For twelve years, Tom was certain his one secretary was doing the work of two.

Instead, two secretaries were doing the work of one—so efficiently, for twelve years, that Tom never suspected.

Two sisters, sharing the same job. Each worked half time. Split the paycheck.

They were identical twins.

27. The Missing Bullet

You want excitement? Visit the first-aid station at one of those big public functions—a county fair, or something like that. Among the child patients you'll find the ones who got sick on the candy, the ones who fell off the rides and even the ones about to be born.

It gets pretty dramatic sometimes. Like that time at the Pan-American Exposition in Buffalo, New York, when they brought in the victim of a shooting.

The victim's name was Bill.

Fortunately for this fellow the first-aid station was a large one, sort of an emergency hospital. They even had an operating room.

And Bill was going to need it! He had taken two bullets at close range.

It was about four-thirty in the afternoon when Bill, conscious yet in severe shock, was taken inside and hoisted to the table and undressed.

It looked bad. The first shot had grazed a rib, had obviously deflected. The second wound was right in the stomach, and there was no exit wound. The bullet was still inside.

The doctors, realizing there was no time to waste, decided to operate. Anesthesia was administered. Bill did not count backward from one hundred. Instead he began, "Our Father which art in heaven, hallowed be thy name. . . ."

In moments he was under.

An incision was made, the abdomen opened. Indeed the bullet had slashed right through the stomach, front and rear walls. The lacerations were sutured—but where was the bullet? Lodged somewhere in the muscles of the back?

It was as though the projectile had vanished.

Cleansing a wound of this kind was imperative, and obviously more than the peritoneal cavity was involved. The doctors really wanted to find that missing bullet, if only to trace its path. Yet this patient, dangerously weakened, might not survive a prolonged probing.

They closed him up—no drainage—and hoped for the best.

Bill was taken to a private residence in Buffalo to recuperate. He did not. A week later, he was dead.

Bill had had a few things going against him—overweight, nearly sixty. Mainly it was that wound, insufficiently cleansed and untraced.

"If" is a big question here, but if the doctors had been able to locate and remove the missing bullet—Bill might have lived.

And this is THE REST OF THE STORY . . .

Bill was shot at the Pan-American Exposition in Buffalo, New York, in 1901. On exhibition at the exposition—apparently unknown to the doctors, and not far from the scene of the shooting—was a new invention, a revolutionary device that could have helped—called the X-ray machine.

That machine—so near yet so far—was operable, and would most certainly have located the fatal bullet.

Instead, Bill—President William McKinley—died with that assassin's bullet inside.

28. Forgotten King

Of England's early kings, he was perhaps the best loved. Yet history has all but forgotten him.

We know that he ruled during the third century.

We know that he ascended to the throne after the death of Asclepiod.

We know that his pleasant nature helped to soothe the savage times in which he lived.

We know that his daughter was a skilled musician.

We know little else.

Today, all that's left of him is an earthwork amphitheater in Colchester . . . and something more. Something which survives the reign of that ancient king to tell us THE REST OF THE STORY.

Historians are not agreed as to when English history begins. Many choose the mid-fifth century as a starting point, if only because this period marks the departure of the Romans from English soil.

Let's go back a bit further.

During Christ's time, England was occupied by an ancient tribe known as the Celts. It would take four centuries for Christianity to be recognized in that northern territory.

In A.D. 43, the Romans invaded England.

Governing the Celts was an easy proposition until the third century. That's the time the Anglos and the Saxons and the Jutes began moving in for a piece of the action.

Among the earliest of those Roman "kings" to defend England against invading tribes was this one in particular. His reign is mentioned briefly by two ancient writers: Geoffrey of Monmouth and Robert of Gloucester.

We see this third-century king as remarkable for his era in that rulers of those days had reputations for negligence, unscrupulousness, thievery and murder.

Not this king.

Geoffrey and Robert characterize him as brave yet even-tempered, as capable yet good-humored. So respected, so popular was he that even his daughter's accomplishments were recorded. Little else is known of this beneficent king.

It is not as though the four centuries during which the Romans ruled England have dropped into obscurity. After all, the fabled King Arthur was one of those early Roman kings. His "Camelot" is under excavation; his life and times are of great interest to scholars.

Yet this other king—the gentle king of the third century —has been all but overlooked in history books.

We do not remember the specific dates of his reign. Nor are the wars in which he fought recounted in prose and poetry.

In fact, we would know nothing of him at all, were it not for the ancient chroniclers Geoffrey and Robert—were it not for the earthwork Roman amphitheater which exists to this day in Colchester—were it not for a few lines of verse written about him.

The third-century author of those lines is unknown. Perhaps he was a court jester or a nobleman—or a man in the street.

Regardless of who is responsible, today we have greater insight into the temperament of an ancient king because someone took the time to make up a rhyme.

In this, the forgotten king has achieved a degree of immortality:

> Old King Cole
> Was a merry old soul,
> And a merry old soul was he.
> He called for his pipe,
> And he called for his bowl,
> And he called for his fiddlers three.

The real—the original—King Cole.

29. Brother Bob

Lula Parker Betenson is ninety-five.

She wants to tell you about her big brother. Seems you're already under a misconception or two about him and she, Lula, wants to make sure that you know THE REST OF THE STORY.

Lula Parker Betenson comes from a Mormon family. Her parents migrated from Iowa to Utah, settled property at Circleville, where Lula still lives.

She had an older brother who died in the thirties; his name was Bob.

In the years since, you've heard a lot about brother Bob Parker. A lot of it isn't true. Lula wants to correct that. She wants you to know him as she knew him.

Bob was a perfect gentleman.

Lula thinks that's important for you to understand.

She remembers Bob's excellent table manners. And that he respected women. And that when dining in a restaurant, he always left a more than appropriate gratuity for the waitress.

These are details, Lula admits, small facets to her brother's overall personality. But together they paint an impressive picture.

Bob adored his mother. When he was away from home, he missed her the most. When he visited, he was so glad to see Mom that he waltzed her around the room. Those memories are most vivid for Lula—Bob dancing joyously with his mother, sweeping her off her feet as if she were a toy and lifting her high into the air.

Folks just don't remember him like that, Lula complains.

They mostly remember the times he sidestepped the law.

Even then, says Lula, it should be recalled that brother Bob never ever killed a man. He was proud of that.

Of course, the emphasis on that fact is not meant to excuse any other wrong he may have done. In fact, when it came to criticism, no one was harder on Bob than Bob.

He was old enough to know better, he always said. He continually reminded himself that what he was doing was shameful and he was always trying very hard to walk the straight and narrow.

Yet, somehow, the straight and narrow was just too straight and too narrow—and Bob would be off again, doing those things he knew he shouldn't be doing.

Bob did not die violently, nor did he die young.

He passed away quietly at a ripe old age in the Pacific Northwest. In bed.

He was not gunned down in South America, as many have come to believe. As a matter of fact, it was the Parker family that helped to sustain that rumor.

For, you see, in the end, Bob did go straight.

Under cover of having supposedly been killed, the last thirty years of his life were peaceful, law-abiding.

Bob might always have been good, his sister Lula assures us. There was simply a time that he fell in with the wrong crowd, a group deservedly called the Wild Bunch.

And of all the bad influences, there was one in particular: a gunslinging horsethief named Harry Longbaugh.

You remember Harry. And you remember Bob, too.

For Lula's brother Bob—the well-mannered gentleman bank robber who found killing distasteful—the mama's boy who tried all his life to be good and finally was—called himself Butch Cassidy.

And his pal, Harry Longbaugh, who tried to keep him on the wrong side of the law—you remember as the Sundance Kid.

30. The Mother of Mother's Day

Anna May Jarvis, quote:

"Mother's Day has nothing to do with candy. Candy is junk. You give your mother a box of candy and then go home and eat most of it yourself. . . ."

Anna May Jarvis, quote:

"A maudlin, insincere printed card or a ready-made telegram means nothing except that you're too lazy to write to the woman who has done more for you than anyone else in the world. You ought to go home and see your mother on Mother's Day. You ought to take her out and paint the town red.   ."

Anna May Jarvis, still quoting now:

"You ought to give her something useful, something permanent. A lot of mothers are sleeping on mattresses that are as hard as rocks. Maybe she needs new eyeglasses, comfortable shoes, a pair of slippers, or better lighting fixtures. Is she sleeping warm at night? Could she use an eiderdown? Maybe the stairs in her home need fixing. . . ."

What about flowers, Anna May?

"Flowers are about half dead by the time they're delivered."

And Anna May goes on to say that she won't rest "until Mother's Day becomes the personal family Memorial Day it was intended to be."

If anyone had the right to speak out against the commercialization of Mother's Day, it was Anna May Jarvis. That second Sunday of thoughtfulness each and every May was Anna's idea in the first place.

Anna May Jarvis was the Mother of Mother's Day. Anna May Jarvis, born May 1, 1864.

She was a minister's daughter, described as a quiet, studious girl in school who liked everyone and whom everyone liked.

Anna was just two weeks forty-two, working for a life insurance company in Philadelphia, when her mother died on the second Sunday of May, 1906.

Friends noticed a change in Anna in the months following that unhappy occasion. No longer the gentle, easygoing woman they knew, Anna became obsessed with but one desire: to see her mother and motherhood honored annually throughout the world.

After more than a year of careful planning, Anna arranged the first Mother's Day church service—May 10, 1908—at St. Andrew's Methodist Church in Grafton, West Virginia, where Anna's mother had taught Sunday school.

Anna worked hard to promote her idea. A year after that first memorial service in West Virginia, Philadelphia became the first city to proclaim an official Mother's Day.

Three years passed.

West Virginia made Mother's Day a statewide observance.

One year later, in 1914, President Woodrow Wilson signed a proclamation from Congress—a document recorded as Public Resolution 25—to establish the second Sunday in May as Mother's Day forevermore.

And it had all begun with Anna. But Anna, now fifty years old, was not content with her victory.

She retired from her job at the insurance company to spend her remaining thirty-four years, and her entire fortune of over a hundred thousand dollars, campaigning against the commercialization of the day she had founded in honor of motherhood.

She interrupted florists' conventions to express her remorse at their "profiteering"; wherever there was a forum for her cause, she spoke out.

Then one day, when she was too old and too tired to

speak out, she was placed penniless, deaf and blind in a West Chester, Pennsylvania, sanitarium.

She died there in November of 1948; she was eighty-four.

And if the story of the woman who invented Mother's Day is made even more poignant, it is by the fact that she, Anna, would never benefit from that time of remembrance.

For Anna May Jarvis—the Mother of Mother's Day, who devoted her life and her fortune to its reverent observance—was never married and was never a mother.

That is THE REST OF THE STORY.

31. The Missing Year

This chapter is the first time THE REST OF THE STORY has ever presumed to tell anybody about a missing year in his own life.

We are doing so only after a careful reading of his biographies, including his own autobiography, and there seems little doubt: one year is missing.

Tom is alive today. He freely, publicly, discusses the intimate details of his life—that he has spent time in a mental hospital, that he is a homosexual.

When, however, he is questioned about one year in particular, he scratches his head, tries to remember, and apparently does not recall. So we're about to open a door which has been closed more than forty years.

In the fall of 1936, Tom entered Washington University in St. Louis.

Among other courses he signed up for English XVI, a course in playwriting. English XVI had quite a good reputation among the students at Washington U. The professor was animated, well liked; the class itself was brimming with enthusiasm and competitive spirit.

Tom somehow just didn't fit in.

Terribly shy, he always wore dark, inobtrusive clothing, sat quietly in the back of the class, socialized with no one.

The highlight of English XVI was a playwriting contest. Each student was to write a one-act play. The plays would be submitted to an independent jury. The jury would then choose three of the plays to be produced by the university dramatic club, and from those three an ultimate winner would be chosen by yet another jury.

There was a great deal of pride and prestige connected with this contest. All the school year, the students of English XVI were hard at work on their one-act plays.

87

Occasionally the professor would read aloud in class fragments of his students' evolving efforts, and finally the professor got around to reading Tom's play.

The play seemed to reflect Tom's brooding personality. It was a dark Russian melodrama full of war and infidelity and jealousy and nightmarish visions and murder.

A polite criticism might have been "heavy-handed." More directly, it was bad. Just plain bad.

In fact, the play was so bad that Tom's usually considerate classmates laughed as it was read aloud by the professor.

Tom did not say a word. Nor did he attempt to alter his lugubrious drama before submitting it to the jury. On the final day of class, the professor announced the names of the three plays which had been chosen. Tom's play was not among them.

Upon hearing this, Tom rose slowly, his face tensed in silent rage, and he left the room.

That was the last they saw of Tom at Washington University.

Today Tom apparently remembers nothing. He does not recall ever having enrolled at Washington U. He does not recall English XVI, nor the contest, nor the rejection of his play, nor even the play itself.

The official University records prove that he was there. His classmates, still living, remember well.

Once upon a time, America's greatest living playwright lost a playwriting contest. He has forgotten that play. And so have we.

We remember *Glass Menagerie.*

We remember *Cat on a Hot Tin Roof.*

We remember *A Streetcar Named Desire.*

In the light of all he's given us since, there's really no need to recall that missing year in the life of Tom . . . "Tennessee" Williams.

32. A Swan Song

Her friends remember her as a warm, joyful and vibrant person, as a woman of everlasting youth who loved amusement parks and French fries and fox-trots and card games.

The rest of the world remembers her as the ethereal maiden in the filmy white costume, as flashing dark eyes and incomparable grace, as the greatest ballerina of all time.

Anna Pavlova.

She lived and loved life, that is true. But so profound was her sense of professional responsibility that she never missed a performance.

Not once.

It is her last performance that concerns us here, in the role for which she is best remembered: the Dying Swan.

Although we may know little of Anna's world, the world of ballet, we'll always remember THE REST OF THE STORY.

In one year alone, Anna gave two hundred and thirty-eight performances in thirty-five weeks, playing seventy-seven towns and cities across the United States. As far as anyone can remember, superstar ballerina Anna Pavlova never missed a performance.

In the course of her career she traveled five hundred thousand miles, dancing before millions of people. This, *before* commercial air travel.

She performed everywhere so that all might enjoy her art. In Jackson, Mississippi, she danced in what amounted to an old garage. There was no stage, only a shallow platform. There were not even dressing rooms, just a few curtains hung in a cellar full of rats.

And Anna performed there, as everywhere, cheerfully. It was as though life itself was so wonderful that there was no room for complaining.

In Montgomery, Alabama, there was a hole in the roof so large that rain poured in, flooding the stage, drenching the costumes and the scenery. Her only remark, after pirouetting through the puddles, was that the dancers needed no stage lights because of the lightning outside.

No, the great Anna Pavlova never missed a performance. It is perhaps because of her perfect record that her ardent admirers never forgot Anna's last scheduled appearance.

It was to be at the Apollo Theater in London, in the role she made famous, the Dying Swan. In that particular role, Anna was known to have surpassed her incredible technique, to have touched her audiences with the compassion of her interpretation.

It was in an atmosphere of unusual excitement that her fans awaited this farewell performance. On the appointed evening at the scheduled time the orchestra began, the curtain rose, the spotlight flashed—and the audience rose to its feet!

All through the performance they stood, gazing into the wandering pool of light.

When it was finished, a raging, thunderous ovation of joy went up, and on, and on.

Even though throughout the performance, the spotlight had brushed—an empty stage!

For this was the ultimate tribute to the indelible artistry of Anna Pavlova. Even in her absence, her audience could see her.

She, only recently fallen ill with pneumonia, could thrill them all—even though she was now two days dead.

33. Dreams of
Ivy Island

Once upon a time, there was a little boy named Phineas
Taylor. He had been born and properly christened in 1810,
in the sleepy parish of Bethel, Connecticut.

One might say that the little boy's dreams began at his
christening. It was then that kindly old Grandfather Taylor
presented newborn Phineas with a deed, a sizable parcel of
land on the outskirts of the parish, a property to which
Grandfather referred as "Ivy Island."

From Phineas's early youth, he was reminded by all with
whom he came in contact that he was a landowner. Young
Phineas was the richest boy in town, his grandfather always
said, for he owned every acre of Ivy Island—the most valuable farm in Connecticut.

Mother and Father, too, frequently reminded Phineas of
his good fortune; they begged him not to forget the rest of
the family when he came of age.

Phineas assured them he would not.

When the neighbors learned that Phineas had inherited
so large a property, they professed to fear that the boy
would refuse to play with their children.

So young Phineas made a point of playing with the
neighbors' children, saying magnanimously that his wealth
would never go to his head.

It did. For while the daydreams of other little boys and
girls were filled with dragons and knights, Phineas's fantasies were based on the reality of his inheritance. One day
he would be the lord of Ivy Island, that promised land of
rippling streams and waving grain upon which Mother Nature had bestowed her finest riches.

Phineas was satisfied with these dreams until the summer

of 1820, when he was ten. It was then that his father gave in to endless pleas and agreed to take young Phineas to see Ivy Island for the first time.

Three sleepless nights preceded the expedition. Then, one bright morning, Phineas and his father and a hired hand began on the long-awaited journey to a young boy's promised land.

Over hill and field Phineas kept inquiring, "How close are we?" And his father would answer that they were very close indeed.

Finally, Dad pointed north to the end of a long meadow and beyond, to a row of tall trees reaching magnificently into the sky.

"There!" he said. "There is Ivy Island!"

Young Phineas, overcome with the joy of anticipation, could wait no longer. He dashed out into the meadow, leaving his father far behind—out to the end of the meadow and to the row of stately trees and to the land which lay beyond.

Ivy Island, the property deeded to Phineas at birth, described by his grandfather as the most valuable farm in Connecticut, was in reality five barren acres of worthless, snake-infested marshland. Struggling ivy vines, clinging for their lives to a few straggling trees in the midst of a dismal swamp. Nothing more.

As the stunned ten-year-old boy continued to gaze upon the shattering dematerialization of his dream, his father and the hired hand who had accompanied them roared with laughter.

For years, young Phineas had been the laughingstock of his family and of his neighborhood, and he had not known until now.

When he returned home, Phineas was soberly congratulated by Grandfather Taylor. The gift of Ivy Island had been the most protracted practical joke the old gentleman had ever staged.

Ten-year-old Phineas was not laughing. Although eventually he forgave, he never forgot.

For that one devastating instance of childhood disillusionment—that one humiliating joke—shaped the rest of Phineas's life.

He became the ultimate con artist, a man determined to prove that the world is full of fools.

Because once he was deceived by his own grandfather, he was inspired to make a lifelong career of deception.

The boy whose fondest hopes once rested in a soggy patch of worthless real estate became the master of the Greatest Show on Earth. The man who boldly declared there to be a sucker born every minute and spent his life proving it, was Phineas Taylor . . . P. T. Barnum.

And now you know THE REST OF THE STORY.

34. A Sex Change for Otto

Harold Gray was born and reared on a farm near Kankakee, Illinois. An excellent student through high school, he went on to Purdue University, graduating in 1917.

World War I. Harold enlisted in the army, served as a bayonet instructor, was promoted to second lieutenant. After the war, he went to work for the Chicago *Tribune*. In 1924, at the age of thirty, Harold Gray seriously considered a sex change.

Not for himself.

For Otto.

Since 1921, Harold had been a member of the Chicago *Tribune* art department. There he had produced the lettering for a comic strip called "The Gumps."

But Harold wanted to strike out on his own. So he invented a cartoon character: Otto. Harold had never attended art school, though his *Tribune* apprenticeship qualified him to handle a comic strip layout.

During the summer of 1924, the aspiring solo cartoonist took a few sketches and a storyboard to the editor of the New York *Daily News*.

The editor took one look at Otto, liked him.

There was a problem, though; something barely definable. The editor took a second, harder look. Then he pegged it.

Otto . . . was effeminate!

The editor's observation startled Hal Gray, and now the cartoonist found himself studying his own art work more closely.

Otto *did* seem a bit feminine.

Of course, the subtle image could be corrected: Otto

could be drawn to appear more masculine.

Again the editor objected. And that is THE REST OF THE STORY.

Gray had been on the right track. He'd simply not gone far enough.

Why not make Otto ultimately feminine? A complete sex change!

The editor further suggested that the heading of the strip be altered to accommodate the metamorphosis of its central character.

Gray had been flirting with the title of a James Whitcomb Riley poem. Now that Otto was a she, the title could be used verbatim.

And that's how it happened.

Within months of its debut—November 2, 1924—Gray's comic strip was a coast-to-coast syndicated smash success.

As the serialized stories developed, threads of violence laced them together.

Gray's cartoon became the object of controversy. Because of one episode which glorified hoodlums, thirty newspapers suspended the strip.

Yet Harold Gray knew what his readers wanted, and they made him many times a millionaire.

He perpetuated his creation personally for forty-five years, until the day he died.

You've forgotten that the comic strip title was borrowed from James Whitcomb Riley. And you never knew that the heroine began as a hero. Until now.

For the cartoon character with whom you fell in love —first in the funnies, now on the Broadway stage—was creatively transformed more than a half century ago, subjected to prepublication pen-and-ink surgery by artist Harold Gray.

And in this way, Little Orphan Otto—became *Little Orphan Annie.*

35. Tell Tail

The accuracy of lie detector tests has never been completely decided upon.

Although it is inadmissible as evidence in court, even the proponents of lie detector testing agree that the tests themselves do not always tell the truth.

Among the very first lie detectors, coincidently considered by some to have been the most accurate, was the donkey's tail!

That's right. In ancient India a suspect would be escorted to a darkened room. Only three would be present: the accused, the interrogator, and a donkey. The person being questioned was told that the donkey would bray if his responses were not truthful, and he was then asked to hold the donkey's tail.

In the 1970s, the lie detector business grew rapidly. More and more companies—banks, stores, warehouses and factories—are using polygraph profiles of their employees. Some firms are now rejecting job applications if the applicant refuses to take a lie-detector test.

Shops and distributors are calling it "shrinkage"; what it is is pilferage. Goods stolen by employees. The Zonn Corporation, the largest polygraph testing outfit in the world, has provided statistics which indicate that shoplifting by shopworkers is at an all-time high and climbing every year.

Of course there is the sometimes inaccuracy of the polygraph itself. Despite the precise multiple measurement of the subject's blood pressure, respiration and electric conductivity of the skin, these measurements will not vary—if the subject actually believes what he says. In other words, if a man really believes that he is Napoleon, a polygraph will *prove* that he is Napoleon!

Forerunners of the modern-day lie detector include a

portable unit, developed in 1930. As early as 1895, an Italian physiologist invented what is called the hydrosphyg-mograph, which simply recorded variation in pulse. Then there were the galvanometer and the pneumonograph. Perhaps none of these early devices was as tried and true, as deadly accurate, as the donkey's tail!

I'm going to run that by for you one more time.

In East India, hundreds of years B.C., when a crime was committed and the suspects apprehended, each suspect was individually submitted to questioning.

He was taken into a darkened room, accompanied only by an interrogator and a donkey.

He was informed that the donkey would bray if a lie was told, and he was asked to hold the donkey's tail.

But the suspect was *not* told that the donkey's tail . . . was covered with black soot!

So those who feared the donkey's telltale bray, in the darkness of the interrogation chamber, dared not touch the donkey's tail. They would emerge with clean hands—GUILTY!

That was THE REST OF THE STORY.

36. Gift of Life

Terry Schafer wanted to buy her husband, David, something special for Christmas.

She dared not tell him what she had in mind, for this particular something special was expensive. If you've ever wanted to surprise your own husband or wife with a gift you really couldn't afford, you'll want to know THE REST OF THE STORY.

September 1977: Terry Schafer is strolling the shops in Moline, Illinois. At a little shop on Fifth Avenue Terry goes inside.

She knows what she's looking for. Her eyes dart eagerly about the shop until they come to rest on a corner display. Terry smiles, walks over to the counter; the shopkeeper looks up, returns her smile.

It's for her husband, Terry explains; it would be a wonderful surprise.

The shopkeeper, nodding, agrees, says this is the very latest, assures her it would be a most appropriate present.

How much? asks Terry.

It's hers, he says, for a hundred twenty-seven dollars and fifty cents. Terry's smile fades into quiet disappointment. David is feeding and clothing them both on a policeman's salary. It is simply too much money. Yet she does so much want it for him.

Then an idea occurs to her: If the shopkeeper would be so kind as to save it for her, to put it away, then perhaps she could pay for it little by little and pick it up before Christmas.

The shopkeeper studies Terry's hopeful expression; no, he will not put it aside for her; neither will he let her leave the store without it.

He will gift-wrap it for her now, he says. She will take it with her. She can pay him later.

Terry just can't be more grateful. She shakes the gentleman's hand, keeps thanking him over and over, telling him how delighted her husband will be.

The shopkeeper says it's nothing. And that's that.

Now it's Saturday, October 1.

Terry's husband, Patrolman David Schafer, working night shift, gets a call on his police radio. A drugstore robbery is in progress.

Officer Dave arrives on the scene just in time to observe the suspect getting into his car, starting the engine, speeding away.

Dave switches on his siren, takes out after the suspect. Three blocks later the getaway vehicle pulls over to the side of the road, stops.

Dave gets out of the patrol car, approaches the suspect, who is still seated behind the wheel of his car.

Now Officer Dave is standing about three feet from the driver's door. The door flies open. The suspect produces an automatic pistol, fires once, sending a .45-caliber slug into Dave's stomach.

At 7 A.M., another patrolman comes to the door of Officer Dave Schafer's home. Wife Terry Schafer answers.

Carefully, calmly, the policeman explains what has happened to her husband. The night before Dave was pursuing a robbery suspect. He has been shot.

As the officer details what's happened to Dave, Terry Schafer is thinking how glad she is that she did not wait until Christmas to give her husband his present, how glad she is that the shopkeeper had been willing to let her pay for it later.

For otherwise, Dave, shot at point-blank range with a devastatingly deadly .45-caliber pistol, would surely have died.

Instead, he was now in the hospital—not with a gunshot wound but with a bruise.

Christmas had come early this year, and Dave had with him the gift of life his wife could not wait to give: his brand-new bulletproof vest.

37. No Coward

He was no coward. He was a spy. He was the man from INTREPID.

During World War II, INTREPID was the code name for Winston Churchill's director of espionage, a man whose real name was William Stephenson. His true identity was known by the enemy, and there was nothing they could do.

Though students of international intrigue will certainly remember Stephenson's brilliant contribution to the Allied cause, they may not recall another fellow, one of Stephenson's star spies.

The man from INTREPID.

This particular agent began his undercover career rather late in the war, and perhaps his most formidable mission was convincing everyone that he was qualified.

First and most difficult to convince of this was Winston Churchill himself. The man from INTREPID spent an interminable time in the Prime Minister's office, trying to impress Churchill with his ideas and his credentials.

He would not be an undercover agent as such, the man from INTREPID explained. He would not be one of those mysterious-looking characters with high black boots and sinister smiles. He would not rely on a false beard, no invisible ink. His handwriting was quite confusing enough when visible, he said.

No, the man from INTREPID would simply be himself.

Fluent in Spanish, he could cover the supposedly neutral Latin American countries. There the Germans were actively preparing their campaigns against the United States.

He would play the Coward, with a capital C, and thereby —hopefully—the enemy would pay little attention to him.

Churchill listened, eventually acquiesced; the man from INTREPID was on his way.

First stop, New York, a meeting with spy-coordinator Stephenson. There was much technical information to be absorbed in a very short time. The man from INTREPID quickly became an expert; the Allies were depending on him.

Surprisingly few Americans knew what he was up to, only the elite of the intelligence network.

With United States senators, the man from INTREPID discussed the war effort. Not one of them realized that he was a spy. Outwardly belittling the Allied attempts at espionage, he sought to throw everyone off his trail. And the subterfuge was successful.

From there, the man from INTREPID traveled abroad. With direct access to influential figures in the so-called neutral countries, he collected opinions, planted rumors.

The slightest trace of political unrest was reported. Gradually the perplexing puzzle of the Nazi underground came together.

"Tiny things are the stuff of intelligence," the man from INTREPID once said. "The smallest details fit into a big picture."

It was in the assembly of these details that the man from INTREPID displayed his genius.

Intrigue was intriguing to him; he could have made a lifetime career as a spy.

He did not.

And you would recognize his name, as everyone then did. But you wouldn't have imagined that he had it in him.

His true profession was so dissimilar, his true nature apparently so unspylike.

When he sang his own witty lyrics on the stage, you applauded. When he acted in the plays he had written, you laughed.

He gave us two hundred and eighty-one songs, including "Someday I'll Find You," "I'll See You Again," "Mad Dogs and Englishmen." As an author of drawing-room comedy, the man with the blithe spirit wrote *Blithe Spirit*; the celebrity with the private life wrote *Private Lives*.

You might have thought him to be gentle. Or perhaps a bit timid. But now you know that he was a coward in name only . . .

Noel Coward. He was THE REST OF THE STORY.

38. Pigeon Problem

During our nation's first century, there was more than a vast westward expanse of wilderness to tame.

America was plagued once by pigeons. From Nova Scotia and Central Quebec, south to Kentucky and west to the eastern edge of the Great Plains, billions of pigeons blackened the sky, blighted the forests.

Frequently their winter migrations took them as far south as Florida, Arkansas, Texas. In 1813, American ornithologist John James Audubon wrote these words after gazing into the Kentucky sky: "The air was literally filled with pigeons. The light of noonday was obscured as by an eclipse . . . and with a noise like thunder they rushed into a compact mass."

Audubon guesstimated more than a billion birds in that single flock, and ornithologists today agree he was probably right.

At one time in the mid-nineteenth century, there may have been as many as nine billion pigeons in the United States alone. That would have been 40 percent of all American birds. In numbers, more than twice the present-day population of human beings on the entire earth.

Whereas most animals require space to survive, those pigeons apparently thrived in a literally stacked-up society. In the forests where millions congregated, branch space eventually ran out until birds were actually standing on top of other birds to form feathered pyramids three feet high. Then the branches would break. Under the enormous weight saplings bent to the ground, and the floor of the forest would fill with pigeon droppings six inches deep.

By the 1860s, news of a flight or nesting of pigeons was flashed to bounty hunters by telegram. And that is THE REST OF THE STORY.

Earning thousands of dollars a week at a penny per bird, pigeon harvesters would swarm to the nesting site. They used sacks and nets and sulphurous fires to asphyxiate the roosting pigeons. Hunters would labor day and night until the woods had been stripped clean.

During one forty-day nesting in Van Buren County, Michigan, eleven million birds were shipped east, three carloads a day.

Feathers were used for mattress stuffing, innards were used for medicine, the meat of the pigeons was eaten. Live birds, as many as twenty thousand at a time, were required for shooting matches.

Now we're going about fifty years ahead in time, to September 1, 1914, to the aviary at the Cincinnati Zoo where Martha, the pigeon, is dying.

Martha has received the best veterinarian care available. She is twenty-nine years old, quite old for a pigeon, and she can hang on no longer.

For fifteen years, since the turn of the century, there had been a standing offer of one thousand dollars to anyone who could provide a mate for Martha.

No mate could be found.

For Martha—like her ancestors about which you've just read, those billions of birds which once flooded the skies of our continent in a great feathery tidal wave—was unique; Martha, and those who had flown before her, were like no pigeons you have ever seen—or will ever see.

For the Passenger Pigeon, with its slate-blue head, gray back and wine-colored breast, whose numbers were so vast that we could not get rid of them fast enough . . . had dwindled down to a solitary bird in a carefully guarded cage: Martha.

There will be some who use the example of her species to demonstrate the vulnerability of an overpopulated society, and others who will shake a finger at shortsighted mankind.

But perhaps as we attack our problems of today, the tale is most eloquently told . . .

On the first of September, 1914, at one o'clock in the afternoon—Martha died. Neither she nor her family will ever pass this way again.

39. Button Up Your Overcoat

Benjamin Harrison was twenty-third president of the United States. You've heard of him. But have you heard of Ben's grandfather, William Henry Harrison?

William Henry was our ninth president. If his name is less familiar, it really shouldn't be, for William Henry Harrison holds a number of records for the presidency:

His 1840 campaign was the first to employ slogans, songs, symbols, parades on a grand scale, all of the modern hoopla.

He was the first president to draw more than a million votes.

He was the first Whig president.

He was, at sixty-eight, the oldest president to be sworn in.

He had more grandchildren, more great-grandchildren, than any other president.

And his inaugural address, one hour and forty minutes long, was the longest ever.

Bill Harrison, as President, was first at something else, too, but that is THE REST OF THE STORY.

William Henry Harrison was born with the proverbial silver spoon in his mouth and he was practically beaten to death with it!

Bill got his start in a three-story brick mansion at Berkeley Plantation. His father had been a signer of the Declaration of Independence and thereafter governor of Virginia.

While some young men would have been content to continue such an elegant life-style, Bill instead fought against the luxury into which he had been born.

He became a soldier. When Bill's future father-in-law

107

asked him how he intended to support the young lady, Bill answered by saying that his *sword* was his means of support.

So the rip-roaring image of William Henry Harrison was well under way.

Remember the slogan "Tippecanoe and Tyler, too"? That was from the 1840 presidential campaign of Bill Harrison and his vice-president, John Tyler. Less memorable were the more significant slogans of that campaign: "Log cabin" and "Hard cider." Those were the symbols of the rough frontier beginnings Bill Harrison longed for but never really had.

For the lack, therefore, of a hard-bitten macho heritage, Bill created one.

To rebel against the three-story brick mansion and the vintage wine, Bill organized mammoth parades with log-cabin floats, massive rallies with free-flowing cider. With that approach Bill won his tooth-and-nail tussle, smashing Martin Van Buren at the ballot box.

The contest was over. The blood-and-thunder was not.

Inauguration day. Cold, damp, blustery.

One of Harrison's horses had been described by John Quincy Adams as particularly mean-looking. Naturally, Bill chose *that* mount to ride from the White House to the Capitol for the outdoor ceremony.

After all, Bill was the Victor. But he was also sixty-eight-year-old Don Quixote.

Disregarding the pleas of staff and family that he wear a hat and topcoat, Bill Harrison made his triumphant ride to the Capitol and stood in the freezing rain for nearly two hours to deliver his all-time record-holding marathon address.

What a man!

Head cold.

Pneumonia.

Thirty-one days later, he was dead.

40. Macie's Grudge

James Macie was illegitimate, a stigma which would cling to him for the rest of his life.

He died wealthy; he died a revered and renowned scientist. But such were the laws of eighteenth-century England that James Macie was denied in life the rights of the most ordinary citizen, denied those rights because of his illegitimacy.

So James Macie held a grudge. A lasting and bitter grudge for the lifelong deprivation of his honor. And we, you and I, benefitted from that grudge in a most remarkable way!

James Macie was born in France in 1765, the illegitimate son of a British duke.

With Jim's father more or less out of the picture, the boy's devoted mother, herself a woman of wealth, returned to England with Jim and immediately set about the task of achieving her son's official acceptance.

She got this far: Jim was decreed a naturalized British subject. Still, because of his illegitimacy, his rights were restricted at almost every turn.

He could not enter Parliament.

He could not hold public office.

He could not hold a job under civil service.

He could not enter the Army, nor the Navy, nor the church.

He could not receive any grants of property at the disposal of the Crown.

Perhaps least fair of all, he could never hold the title of his true father, the Duke of Northumberland.

Jim grew up knowing those restrictions. Maybe that accounts for his desire to excel at everything. Whatever the motivation, he did excel.

In 1786, Jim graduated from Pembroke College and shortly thereafter launched himself upon a scientific career.

Many sophisticated experiments and published results later, Jim became a respected scientist. While his scientific colleagues, no more talented than he, were being knighted for their accomplishments, Jim was denied that honor. Through no fault of his own, but because he was born illegitimate.

It is no wonder that James Macie held a grudge.

He vowed never to marry, realizing that the stigma of illegitimacy would pass to his children. Yet in his lifetime James Macie conceived another form of immortality. And the idea in itself would serve as his personal rejection of the country which had rejected him.

When Jim died in 1829, he died a wealthy man with no heirs who could claim his vast fortune. In his will he sought revenge on England by leaving all of his money . . . to the United States of America!

Jim had never even visited the United States. Yet by willing his fortune to us, he disinherited England as it had disinherited him.

In his will he specified that his money was to be used for the foundation of an establishment which would increase and diffuse knowledge among men and which would perpetuate his true family name, denied him at birth. The name he adopted later in life. The name Smithson.

And thus, the gift he gave us—the establishment which in reality represents the torment of illegitimacy—is today our country's most magnificent storehouse of cultural and scientific accomplishment.

It is called the Smithsonian Institution.

And now you know THE REST OF THE STORY.

41. The Volunteer

Dr. Evan O'Neill Kane was chief surgeon of Kane Summit Hospital in New York City. At age sixty he had been a surgeon for thirty-seven years. Like most physicians of great experience, Dr. Kane had become preoccupied with a particular facet of medicine.

His strong feelings concerned the use of general anesthesia in major surgery. Dr. Kane believed that most major operations could and should be performed under local anesthesia, for in his opinion the hazards of general anesthesia outweighed the risks of the surgery itself.

For example, Dr. Kane cited the surgical candidate with a history of heart trouble. In such a case, a surgeon may be reticent to operate fearing the effects of the anesthesia on the heart.

And of course there were those patients with specific anesthesia allergies who never awakened. Dr. Kane's medical mission was to prove to his colleagues the viability of local anesthesia in most surgical procedures. And it would take a great deal of convincing.

Many patients were understandably squeamish at the thought of being "awake while it happens." Others feared the possibility of the anesthetic wearing off during surgery.

To break down these psychological barriers Dr. Kane would have to find a volunteer, a candidate for major surgery who would be willing to accept local anesthesia.

Someone did volunteer. He is THE REST OF THE STORY.

In his distinguished thirty-seven-year medical career Dr. Evan Kane had performed nearly four thousand appendectomies, so this next appendectomy would be routine in every way but one: Dr. Kane's patient would remain awake throughout the surgery under local anesthetic.

111

The operation was scheduled for Tuesday morning, February 15.

The patient was prepped, wheeled into the O.R. Local was administered.

Dr. Kane began as he had thousands of times before, carefully dissecting superficial tissues and clamping blood vessels on the way in.

Locating the appendix, the sixty-year-old surgeon deftly pulled it up, excised it and bent the stump under.

Through it all the patient experienced only minor discomfort.

The operation concluded successfully.

The patient rested well that night, and the following day his recovery was said to have progressed beyond that of the typical postoperative patient.

On the afternoon of the seventeenth, just two days after his surgery, the patient was released from the hospital to recuperate at home.

Dr. Kane had proved his point.

The risks of general anesthesia could be avoided in major operations; the potential of local anesthesia had been fully realized—thanks to the example of an innovative doctor and a brave volunteer.

Oh, did I mention that this milestone surgery was performed February 15 . . . 1921? And did I mention that Dr. Evan O'Neill Kane and the patient who volunteered for the experimental procedure had a great deal in common?

They were the same man.

Dr. Kane—to prove the viability of local anesthesia in major surgery—had operated on himself!

42. Alive!

None of us wants to feel stranded on an island of Now in an ocean of Time, but it is the Japanese in particular whose hunger for the continuity of life has motivated painstaking backtracking through time.

In fact as well as in fiction.

Japan's motion picture industry was the first to resurrect prehistory in the form of Godzilla, Rodan. In fact, Japan's scientists have dared to retrace man's tiny footprints back to the enormous ones of his predecessor monsters.

It was in the mud and slime of a peat bog, in a Kemigawa farmyard twenty-five miles southeast of Tokyo, that a team of workmen found what they were *not* looking for . . .

Alive!

And that brings us to THE REST OF THE STORY.

The workmen had been digging in a peat deposit not far from Tokyo. They had found something important. That's how a team of archaeologists heard it; that's why they rushed to the scene.

How far down? a workman was asked.

Eighteen feet.

The fossilized remains of a canoe, and something else. One of the archaeologists climbed into the pit, reached down, parted the soil with his hands. Then, crying out, he drew back!

Others converged.

Breathless moments passed. It was agreed that only one scientist in all of Japan would be qualified to carry on from there. Dr. Ichiro Ohga.

Dr. Ohga was notified, was rushed from Tokyo to the excavation site.

113

As he peered down into the bog, as his eyes fell on its secret, his pulse quickened.

"My God, is it dormant? Or is it possibly . . . alive?"

The scientists were not afraid for themselves. All their lives they had trained and preconditioned themselves for surprise. But they knew that this find must somehow be removed promptly to some safe place—lest it should come to life.

They had heard of the giant reptiles discovered in peat bogs, the mastodons trapped in sheets of ice with skin, organs, everything, preserved. But never before was there this degree of hope that something might be discovered from thousands of years past, still living!

We do not know the details of how their find was removed to the safety of a laboratory.

We know that it got there. We know that Dr. Ohga kept a round-the-clock vigil, and we know that in four days, under laboratory-created climatic conditions, perceptible movement!

Cameramen were summoned to record this unprecedented resurrection. Japan's scientific community was alerted to the surprise that there was life left over from the time when Roman legions first invaded England. A living thing had survived from *prehistoric* Japan. The chain of unbroken links which comprised Oriental psychology, sociology, philosophy and theosophy had led a living thing from the lifeless past to join them in the present.

For the discovery in a peat deposit, eighteen feet below the earth, cradled in the fossilized remains of a canoe— a two-thousand-year-old ungerminated, dormant, apparently lifeless . . . *seed.*

And after four days, a sprout; after fourteen months, a delicate, pink lotus flower.

The seed that went to sleep when Jesus did . . . was awake!

43. Practice Run

Bill Turner lived the nineteenth-century tradition of the sea.

As a lad he longed to feel the waves beneath him, the stinging ocean air in his face.

So he ran away from home to become a cabin boy on a merchant vessel. Bill Turner was what—sixteen at the time?

The captain smiled to see the scrawny young fellow lugging his belongings up the gangplank in a leather shoulder sack. Perhaps he saw himself as a boy, running away to sea to imagined adventure.

But for young Bill Turner, imagined adventure and reality would become one.

Soon.

At noon, Bill watched the naked masts and spars, magnificently attired, tugging against the gleaming white billow. Then the deck rocked free and the old ship, shed of its mooring, drew out to sea.

Bill was where his heart would always be—at sea!

That night he lay awake in his bunk, listening to the older seamen singing chanties. The ship groaned and creaked its dysrhythmic accompaniment as the waves sloshed gently at her hull. For the thrilling newness of it all, Bill could not sleep.

First stop on the voyage: Kinsale Harbor, Ireland. They were due in the morning.

But they would never reach it in one piece. In the predawn dark, gale winds whipped up a mile from port. Within the hour, tempest velocity.

The old ship twisted and pitched, alerting all hands.

By the time every man had made his station it was too late. Young Bill Turner arrived on deck just as the main and the mizzen snapped in half like stems of straw.

Abandon ship was called. The hull was about to rupture. And Bill Turner, the cabin boy, on the first night of his first voyage, jumped overboard and swam for his life.

The icy water made his muscles contract. He struggled against the waves, adrenalin fighting the cold, craning his neck to clear the big rollers.

One thought was fixed in his mind. Swim for shore. Swim for Ireland.

As the dawn broke, the sea calmed. Bill found himself clinging to a rock on the coast. The peril was past. For a while. And that is THE REST OF THE STORY.

For Bill Turner did not give up the sea.

He would be Captain William Turner one day. And one night fifty years in the future, the last night of his last voyage would be like the first night of his first.

Again he would be shipwrecked off the coast of Ireland, off the same Old Head of Kinsale.

Again he would jump into the icy water to relive the fear of a young cabin boy.

And again, aged by fifty years and though far from shore, he would swim for Ireland. Instinctively. As he had fifty years before.

Had he not, he would have gone down with the rest. The passing ship would never have picked him up.

Bill Turner's life was saved because he had a practice run fifty years before he became captain . . . of the *Lusitania!*

44. Abe Lincoln Story

You thought you had heard all the Abe Lincoln stories. It is unlikely that you have read this one.

When Abraham Lincoln was living in Washington County, he was captured by the Indians.

He was working a farm there and the Indians, angered by the fact that Abe was encroaching on their territory, captured him, made him run between two rows of braves. As Abe ran, the braves beat him with sticks, a humiliation known as "running the gauntlet."

Of course you know that Abe survived. You know that he was assassinated many years later.

But when he escaped from the Indian camp he fled to Rockingham County, perhaps because he was genuinely repentant for having settled on Indian land or perhaps because he was just plain frightened.

At any rate, a year or two went by. The nightmare of his experience in Washington County continued to haunt him, to eat away at him. The more he thought about it, the more certain he became: The land he had abandoned was his home and it had been cowardly to run away.

So Abe made up his mind once and for all. He would return to Washington County, to the little farm he had left. He would claim it once again, and this time he would not forsake it.

Four years passed. He split rails and planted crops and harvested them. Four years, no trouble with the Indians.

And then one day, Abe was clearing a patch of forest to open a new field. At the top of its arc, the ax blade gleamed in the brilliant sunlight. The air was clean and fresh, laden with the pleasant aroma of green wood and wildflowers and freedom.

No more would he lie awake at night, fearing the wrath

of the Indians. No more would he be consumed in self-doubt. Abe had finally stood up for what he believed. This land was his now. No one was going to take it away from him.

But each time Abe's ax chunked into the side of the tree, it obscured another sound. One footstep . . . followed by another . . . and another . . .

A hundred yards away, drawing closer, a lone Indian brave! Camouflaged in forest-colored buckskin, the Indian crept up carrying a long-barreled firearm of the white man.

He had been sent on this mission by his tribe, to journey to the Lincoln farm and to kill Abe Lincoln.

Abe continued to chop the tree. Stealthily the brave made his way through the forest, treading on the swatches of grass, avoiding the dry twigs which might alert his prey.

A sudden rustle in the treetops, a squirrel jumping from one limb to another. Abe glanced up . . . then back to his work. As Abe raised his ax again, the blade glistened once more.

The Indian lowered the barrel of his gun, took aim . . . and fired!

Abe Lincoln felt the sting of the bullet in his back and fell to the ground. He looked up just in time to see an Indian brave disappear into the forest.

Only a moment of consciousness was left, and within minutes—Abraham Lincoln was dead.

Abraham Lincoln was dead and from a nearby clearing his eight-year-old son, Thomas, had seen it all.

When Thomas grew up he named his son after his father, and Thomas's son—also named Abraham Lincoln—became the sixteenth president of the United States.

President Abraham Lincoln and his grandfather both had sons named Thomas. Both had wives named Mary.

And both were felled by an assassin's bullet.

And now you know THE REST OF THE STORY.

45. The Cabinet
in the Nursery

Perhaps young Bob's parents should not have told him about the cabinet in the nursery. That it had been made by William Brodie.

Oh, the cabinet itself was a fine old piece of furniture, an elaborately carved, handcrafted antique. But the same hands which had so skillfully fashioned it had also carried twin pistols into a series of daring crimes.

Brodie was eventually captured, charged with armed robbery and murder, tried, convicted and hanged.

Some seventy years later the wooden cabinet he made sat in a corner of Bob's nursery, inspiring an endless stream of childhood daydreams.

And one nightmare.

Bob grew up, and grew up to become a writer—but he never forgot the cabinet in his nursery, the one made by outlaw William Brodie. It was THE REST OF THE STORY.

Just what was the fuss about Bad Bill Brodie?

He was a depraved character of the eighteenth century who lived in Edinburgh, Scotland, Bob's hometown. He was a heavy drinker and a heavy gambler; his comrades were thieves and his haunts were the lowest dives in the city.

At first Brodie worked alone in his criminal activities. In time, he organized a gang comprised of himself and three ex-cons. Together they shared cheap wine, expensive women and lascivious merriment, terrorizing Edinburgh as they went. In 1788, Brodie was hunted down and captured.

They threw the book at Bad Bill Brodie, a gamut of felony charges running from armed robbery to murder. He was tried, convicted, executed.

There his story might have ended, were it not for Bob.

As a child, Bob had spent many hours gazing at the cabinet in his nursery and listening to the strange tale of the outlaw who had made it.

As an emerging writer, aged fifteen, Bob had become so fascinated by the life of William Brodie that he wrote a play about him. But something did not fit. The character had not yet come to life on paper. Reconstructing, rewriting, did not seem to help.

When Bob was thirty-five, married, successful, he was home in bed, asleep one night, but his rest was not peaceful.

Bob's wife awakened to hear her husband screaming. She shook him. He opened his eyes, sitting bolt upright in bed, and still trembling he related his nightmare to her.

It had been about a man, a man very much like outlaw William Brodie. Only the rogue in his dream had seemed so real and so horrible.

The next morning, Bob began to write. Three days and some forty thousand words later, he was finished.

Although you may never have heard of Bad Bill Brodie, you know well the character he inspired that poured from Bob's prolific pen, a sinister synthesis spun from a shadowy web of facts and dreams.

You will better understand writer Bob's fascination when you come to know the other side of the real Bill Brodie. For it is true that he was a libertine, a nefarious criminal, the scourge of Edinburgh. But all those things he was . . . he was by night.

By day, William Brodie was a respected businessman, a much-admired member of the Edinburgh Town Council, the president of his union, a pillar of the highest society, a deacon. Oh, yes—and a cabinetmaker.

It was the dual nature of Deacon Brodie—the two incongruous, unrelated human halves—that haunted Bob's dreams, eventually to inspire one of literature's most unforgettable characters.

For, in a way, the doors of a handmade nursery cabinet opened wide so that one day, a young man named Bob— Robert Louis Stevenson—could relate to you *The Strange Case of Dr. Jekyll and Mr. Hyde.*

46. Stairway
to Heaven

A block south of La Fonda Hotel in Santa Fe, New Mexico, on the corner of Water Street and Old Santa Fe Trail, there is an iron-fenced courtyard. Open the gate. Pass through the courtyard. Enter the Gothic chapel. And when your eyes adjust to the candlelight you will not believe what they see.

No one does.

One hundred and twenty-seven years ago, in the fall of 1852, the Roman Catholic sisters of Loretto left Kentucky and crossed the continent to establish a convent in the southwestern desert.

The ancient village to which they traveled, founded by the Spanish in 1610, was known as the City of the Holy Faith. Today La Villa de la Santa Fé is Santa Fe, New Mexico.

Some two decades after the sisters arrived, Mexican carpenters began to construct a chapel for them. It was to be patterned after the Sainte-Chapelle in Paris, Gothic in architecture, with a choir loft at the rear.

Construction started in July of 1873. Five years later Loretto Chapel was completed. Almost. The chapel sanctuary was magnificent, including the choir loft. But there was no way to get from one to the other. The builders, confounded by the architectural dilemma of rising so high in so small a space, had omitted a stairway! Their ladder, while adequate for workmen, was both unbecoming and hazardous for the sisters and the singers.

In the years that followed, many carpenters were consulted. All gave the same answer: a conventional stairway to the choir loft would take up too much room in the chapel below.

The sisters of Loretto, who had traveled thousands of miles to establish their convent, in the face of what appeared to be their first insurmountable difficulty, took their problem to their knees.

A novena to St. Joseph.

It was on the ninth day, the last day of the novena, that a gray-haired man leading a donkey and carrying a tool chest came to town and stopped at the convent academy

To the Mother Superior, the old man said he had learned of their problem, that they needed a stairway to their chapel choir loft. Perhaps he could help.

He was welcome to try, the mother superior said.

Using only the crudest tools, the old man went to work. He was eight months painstakingly applying his obvious skill and his primitive tools.

And then one morning, the Mother Superior awakened to find the job completed, and the carpenter—gone.

As the sisters congregated in the chapel that morning, each stood silent and wide-eyed before an incredible masterwork.

The staircase was a narrow, graceful spiral of thirty-three steps. Two complete three-hundred-and-sixty-degree turns. No bannister. No center support. Precision-fit, meticulously held together with barely perceptible wooden pegs richly polished, a spiral that was beautiful to the point of seeming alive.

But where was the carpenter? He had not yet been paid for his work and was nowhere to be found. Nor had the local lumber supplier any record of wood having been purchased for the project.

Builders and engineers who have examined the staircase affirm that its full weight appears to rest at its base. Structurally, it should have collapsed the first time it was used. Yet it has been used every day . . . for a hundred years.

And here is "a strange": Though it was built on the spot, the unidentified hardwood, whatever it is, is from nowhere near New Mexico.

Although the present-day sisters of Loretto are reticent to be specific, they are satisfied that the gray-haired carpenter who came to town one day a century ago, whoever he was, came in answer to their prayers to the patron saint of carpenters. And that his stairway, in one way, does not end at the choir loft . . . but leads beyond the stars.

And now you know THE REST OF THE STORY.

47. The Escapist

Ed . . . was going mad. Had Ed been born into an age of flourishing psychiatry, he would have been a candidate for the couch.

Instead, and especially because he was quiet about his approaching insanity, Ed was left to his own devices.

He was born in Chicago in 1875. A born loser.

His parents had been wealthy enough to send him to the most fashionable prep schools in the Midwest and East. Ed flunked out of all of them.

Now, at nineteen, things got worse. Ed's father went broke, died the same year, leaving Ed orphaned and penniless.

Ed got a job as a cattle drover. Fired.

Ed went to work as a railroad policeman. Fired.

Then he became a law clerk. Fired.

He tried his hand at door-to-door peddling. No one wanted anything . . . from Ed.

Then he went to work for Sears, Roebuck as an office stenographer. He was fired from that job too.

Now it was plain that Ed had been thinking too small. The only way he was ever going to succeed was to go into business for himself. Then he would be his own boss. No one could fire him.

So he went into business for himself.

Bankrupt.

Within the year after Ed's advertising agency went down the drain, he started his own correspondence school for young men who wanted to learn "how to succeed in business"!

It is easy to surmise what happened to *that* venture. At thirty-seven, Ed was back where he started. Penniless and a failure.

Ed, despondent over a wasted life, started talking to himself. A little bit, at first. Then a lot.

In another fifty years it might have been fashionable to seek out psychiatric help, to lie on a couch and relate fantasies to an analyst. Instead, Ed related his fantasies to himself. Aloud.

Each evening, for an hour or two, Ed told himself weird stories, creating strange plots and stranger characters as he went along.

If anyone had overheard Ed telling himself what it was like under the moon of Mars and such, Ed might have been confined as mentally ill.

But Ed kept his private storytelling sessions private.

No one would know about his fantasies, until one day he started writing them down. That is THE REST OF THE STORY.

For Ed, the flat-broke failure who turned everything he touched to ashes, had not yet tried one thing.

Perhaps on the very brink of insanity, his tortured mind instead went to work for him, creating dozens of forgettable stories.

And one *un*forgettable one.

A story about a place he had never visited, of which he knew nothing, and about a character who existed only in the private fantasy world of Edgar Rice Burroughs . . . Tarzan. Tarzan of the Apes.

48. Jacob's Medical Milestone

We thought Julius Caesar was the first. He was not. I'm referring to children given birth by what we now call Caesarian section, the procedure of surgically removing a newborn infant from its mother's womb.

Tradition has it that Julius Caesar was born this way; no historian will stake his reputation on it.

The first recorded Caesarian section, by which both mother and baby survived, was performed in Switzerland in 1500 by a man named Jacob.

His accomplishment was a medical milestone, his skill most remarkable for his day. Necessity was the mother of his invention, for he accepted a case no one else would take.

According to ancient Greek mythology Aesculapius was cut from the body of his dead mother by the sun god, Apollo. That was the legendary precedent for Caesarian section, later to be repeated in fable and in reality.

Until 1500, however, Caesarian section was at best a half-successful operation. Even when the child was saved, the mother, in order to qualify for surgery, was usually already dead.

A.D. 1500. Only eight years before, the world was believed flat and now a modern surgical procedure was about to be demonstrated. The subject's name was Frau Nufer.

Mrs. Nufer was an attractive young Swiss woman, apparently healthy in every way. There was no indication that her labor was to be a difficult one.

It was. With the child overdue, Mrs. Nufer was bedridden in agony for days. Her midwives panicked, summoned surgeons.

In keeping with the medical practices of the dawning sixteenth century, Mrs. Nufer's physicians refused to perform the surgery which might save her life . . . because she was not yet dead. It was better this way, they said. At least her unborn child would have a chance.

There was one in their midst who disagreed; his name was Jacob.

Mrs. Nufer did not have to die, he told the others. She was young and strong. An operation might be performed before a crisis had been reached, thus saving both the mother and the baby.

Incensed at this suggestion and not wishing to be considered accomplices in the murder of Mrs. Nufer, the conformist physicians left the room. Jacob was alone with the frightened midwives and the delirious mother. It was the longest long shot in the world, never before attempted.

Jacob would try with a confident ease to mask his own apprehension as he removed the instruments from his bag. If he succeeded, he would be a hero. If he failed, he would be an assassin.

Within the hour, Jacob emerged from Mrs. Nufer's room . . . a hero.

His patient was alive, safe, resting comfortably, as was her newborn child.

The surgical success achieved by Jacob in 1500 would not be repeated with frequency and safety until the development of modern anesthetics and antiseptics. So Mrs. Nufer was lucky.

She lived to bear other children without complications, dying at the age of seventy-seven.

Beyond the skill of Jacob and the luck of his patient, there was another factor. Another something special doubtless influenced the outcome of this remarkable operation, the first documented successful Caesarian. That something was love.

For Jacob was not a doctor at all. He was the woman's

husband, the child's father. And Jacob Nufer's surgical instruments were equipment for gelding sows.

His profession: hog butcher.

That was THE REST OF THE STORY.

49. Rescue Party

Jamestown was the first English settlement in America. That is the way we have always heard it and that is the way it was.

We were also taught that three shiploads of English settlers, a hundred and four men, had been sent to the New World by the London Company to organize a trade base.

They were and it was.

The hope of finding gold and silver was also a prime incentive for the eager colonists.

What else do the history books say?

They were five months at sea before reaching Chesapeake Bay in April of 1607; they were seventeen days on the James River before deciding upon a site for their settlement. And it was not a good choice.

The location was low and swampy.

The food supply was limited, the drinking water virtually undrinkable.

Malaria struck.

Indians struck.

Bad weather struck.

It was like colonizing the moon, with none of the advantages.

But did we learn the *real* trouble which almost caused the mission to abort?

The problem with Jamestown, and how it was solved, is THE REST OF THE STORY.

Jamestown Colony was barely a year old, and in trouble.

Settlement leader Captain John Smith had the primary problem pegged precisely: his company was comprised of gentleman adventurers, temperamentally ill prepared to meet the adversity which lay before them.

In an urgent message to his sponsors back home, Captain Smith said: Send me some *men!*

Send carpenters, blacksmiths and masons. I would rather have a handful of those than a thousand like those I have.

September 25, 1608, the handful from London sailed up the James River.

The ship *Good Speed* brought six broad-shouldered workmen to Jamestown. *Work*men.

A rescue party.

Axes slung over their shoulder, the new men followed Captain Smith into the forest in search of a likely area to make a clearing.

Within three weeks a plot had been cleared, a furnace had been erected. The workmen tapped pine trees and began distilling tar and pitch.

It was the first factory in the New World.

The rescue party then proceeded to set up a soap works and a saw mill. By November 1608, a little more than a month after the six workmen had arrived in Jamestown, the other colonists became inspired by the splendid example and were themselves hard at work.

According to Captain John Smith, the first English foothold in the New World was saved—specifically—by six able men.

Because of them, the English colony of Jamestown survived:

> Michal Lowicki
> Zbigniew Stefanski
> Jur Mata
> Jan Bogdan
> Karol Zrenica
> Stanislaw Sadowski

For the six men who rescued Jamestown, the six enthusiastic workers who taught the English how to work—were Polish.

That was twelve years before the *Mayflower* landed!

50. Surprise Attack

Beginning in 1931 and for the next decade, the same question appeared on every final exam for each graduating class at Japan's Naval Academy.

Now what would that be?

For ten years, every graduating naval cadet in Japan was asked the same question: "How would you carry out a surprise attack on Pearl Harbor?"

When that question first appeared on the exam, there was no correct answer. Then in February of 1932, nine years and ten months prior to the real attack on Pearl Harbor, the Japanese discovered what they believed was a foolproof plan.

That strategy was in fact the one they eventually employed.

Yet for nine years more, the question "How would you carry out a surprise attack on Pearl Harbor?" appeared on the Japanese Naval Academy final.

With literally hundreds of various suggestions, gleaned from the fertile minds of Japanese youth, not one could rival the strategy of 1932.

How they really surprised us at Pearl is THE REST OF THE STORY.

In the fall of 1941, a Japanese ship arrived at Honolulu. Four members of the crew, who were posing as stewards, were really officers in the Japanese Imperial Navy. Two submarine experts, two surface ship and air operations experts.

Had we been more suspicious at the time, we might have wondered why that particular ship had taken the route it did to the islands. A far-north approach, passing near the icy Aleutians.

Today we know that the four Japanese naval experts

were testing a plan the Japanese had been counting on for almost ten years. Much to their gratification, the Japanese naval officers sighted neither ships nor aircraft on this desolate swath of sea.

A month later a fleet of Japanese ships would take this same route to Hawaii, only then it would be for real.

The Japanese officers, disguised as stewards, took plenty of shore leave, saw the sights, took snapshots, spoke with the island natives. They even took tourist plane rides over Pearl Harbor—and more snapshots.

They were testing a plan—and so far, the plan was on target.

The consulate gave these Japanese "stewards" maps of Pearl Harbor and the military airfields. Just to make certain, they purchased souvenir sets of picture postcards containing aerial shots of Pearl, views of Battleship Row and the mooring area by Ford Island.

Returning to Japan, the naval officer spies were confident; the plan they had had for a decade was the right one.

Indeed, it was the plan they used December 7, 1941— and were we surprised!

In 110 minutes, 8 big battleships and 3 light cruisers had been sunk or damaged, 188 planes had been destroyed, 2400 men had been killed.

The blow not only paralyzed us in the Pacific for the greater part of a year, it also exposed our inexcusable optimism and our unbelievable unreadiness for battle.

Behind our anger was one burning question: How did they do it?

Before 1950, six investigations were launched in search of an answer.

The Japanese plan of attack was more than theory: it had been proved effective. For in 1932, U.S. Admiral Harry Yarnell decided to demonstrate the vulnerability of Pearl Harbor by slipping two aircraft carriers in close

from the northeast. He launched 152 aircraft which theo-
retically could have obliterated all airplanes on the ground
and sunk most of the ships at anchor.

Japanese naval attaches in Honolulu read about the
exercise, were so impressed that they filed voluminous dis-
patches to Tokyo.

Their report ultimately manifested itself as the Japanese
Master Plan.

That's right.

Almost a decade before the attack on Pearl Harbor, *we*
showed the Japanese how!

51. Shorty

It's azalea time in Tyler, Texas, during late March and early April. Let's take a walk downtown, down Broadway. Here we are at the courthouse. In 1954, when this courthouse was built, you couldn't find more modern architecture anywhere. The building is four stories high, has two wings on either side. Lots of long windows.

Broadway, the street we're walking, used to end here. These two blocks, the one where the courthouse sits and the plaza across the street, were one big Texas-size block some while ago.

Let's walk a bit farther. The courthouse plaza has never been more lovely. The azaleas are a symphony of color.

You see the concrete square in the middle? From time to time you'll see an art fair there. Or a celebration of the Veterans of Foreign Wars. Or Santa Claus at Christmastime. The trees here are mostly stately, shapely pin oaks. An occasional cherry tree.

There's one holly tree in the plaza. There is a grave beneath it. And that is THE REST OF THE STORY.

Over there it is. Impressive slant marker. Georgia marble.

No epitaph. Just a name, and the dates of birth and death.

When he lived folks called him "Shorty." Surely you would expect the only grave in the Tyler, Texas, courthouse plaza to be that of a prominent citizen like a beloved mayor or a war hero.

But, no, that place of honor is reserved for an otherwise ordinary local character, a panhandler who died penniless.

Nobody in East Texas would ever have called Shorty what he was. A beggar is what he was.

What citizen of Tyler, shop clerk or city official, was not

familiar with Shorty's face? For almost fifteen years he frequented the courthouse area.

Shorty's memory went way back to the years before the new courthouse was built. After the new one was built, after Broadway intersected the park and made a plaza, seeing old Shorty and saying hello somehow kept folks in touch with the way things once were.

Those last years were the hardest for Shorty, when his eyes started to go.

But you know what?

By then the aging panhandler had become such a beloved personality in Tyler that the town awarded him free medical care. They even slowed the speed limit on Broadway and designated a reserved pedestrian crossing zone especially for Shorty.

Even up to the last, the media in its editorials always considered how Shorty felt about this issue and that.

Shorty's closest friends were the old-timers who hung around the plaza. He outlived many of them.

The end came August 5, 1963.

Of course, Shorty's death made local headlines, merited multicolumn newspaper stories with touching photos of the departed.

Naturally, there was a crowd for his funeral.

Shorty's final resting place was officially determined to be the courthouse plaza—really the only home he ever knew. He is there still, sleeping peacefully beneath a holly tree, amid the splendor of the azaleas.

There lies Shorty, the American Southwest's most famous squirrel.

52. The Secret
of the Oneida

The details of a long-forgotten medical file go back to late spring 1893.

The patient notices a sore spot in his mouth. Specifically, on the roof of his mouth.

Weeks pass; the sore does not heal. To the contrary, it is either becoming more noticeable or actually more inflamed.

The patient consults his family physician.

The physician makes an examination, determines the presence of a sizable growth, fears the worst.

The doctor's orders: The growth must be removed at once.

June 30. A surgeon has been selected: Dr. W. W. Keen.

That evening the patient is admitted to special preoperative quarters for the night. No sedative is administered.

Next morning, July 1, the patient is taken to quarters which have been modified for the purpose of surgery.

The patient is fifty-six years old, overweight. Although under general anesthesia he will run the risk of stroke, the duration and the magnitude of this particular surgery demand that the risk be taken.

Nitrous oxide is indicated, administered; the patient remains semiconscious.

Switch to ether.

The patient is under now; his pulse is regular, strong.

The upper bicuspid teeth on the left side are removed; incisions are made in the palate; the growth is exposed.

The worst is confirmed.

The tumor is identified as carcinoma.

Cancer has involved the entire antrum sinus cavity. The

tumor must be excised and surrounding tissue removed.

Not even the left side of the jaw may be spared if the possibility of recurrence is to be held to a minimum.

The operation is considered a success.

An artificial jaw is prepared for use after recuperation.

A case-history follow-up: The cancer does not recur and the patient does recover to enjoy a healthy normal life of fifteen years more.

When he dies, it is at the age of seventy-one of a heart attack.

And now it can be told, eighty-five years after that remarkable surgery, that the operation took place—not in a hospital—but aboard the *Oneida.* A privately owned yacht!

It is difficult to recall the days of discretion, before we demanded that our heroes be human, before the tabloid preoccupation with the arrest records of celebrities.

In recent times, though we still vote for the invincible, we later incongruously require of our elected leaders— vulnerability. We demanded the details of Eisenhower's stroke and Kennedy's bad back. Such was our voyeuristic pleasure that Lyndon Johnson was compelled to expose his surgical scar on the White House lawn.

Whether our present public attitude is progress or regress is yours to decide. Still the record shows that in the early summer of 1893, a candidate for surgery so prized his privacy that he boarded a friend's yacht in the dead of night, submitted to the operation the next morning after the vessel had set sail. The incident was not fully revealed until twenty-five years later, long after the patient's death.

The patient was President Grover Cleveland.

Now you know THE REST OF THE STORY.

53. His Biggest Fan

Surely no figure throughout the twentieth-century politics
of Italy wielded more power nor held greater fascination
for the people of that country than did Benito Mussolini.

Il Duce, they called him. "The Leader."

Significantly his charisma was that of a matinee idol
rather than that of a statesman, though his was a charm
bathed in blood. Requests for autographed photographs
were not at all uncommon.

This relates to one such request which was denied to a
young fan of Mussolini's.

Would Il Duce have signed and sent that photograph
had he known THE REST OF THE STORY?

The popular appeal of Benito Mussolini was phenomenal. Having transformed Italy into a choreography of uni-
forms, parades, martial music and punctual trains, he had
laid the groundwork for the respect of those under his
leadership. Yet Il Duce wanted more than respect.

Short, strapping, square-jawed, he was not the physical
prototype of a romantic hero. At the height of his power
he was neither young enough to play the role of Alexander
the Great nor old enough to be regarded as venerable.

Mussolini's charisma could not be defined in conventional terms.

A self-styled political pope, he greeted throngs of wor-
shippers from his balcony. Parents held their children up
so they could see. That he had captured the imagination
of Italian youth was one of his strongest advantages. To
young men he represented the ideals of manhood; to young
women he was seduction and security in one, a sex symbol.

So Il Duce was much more than the title implies; he was
a master of public relations, a superstar of the first magnitude. In the maintenance of his celebrity he was perhaps

more conscientious than he need have been. Yet on one occasion he dealt rather abruptly with a young admirer.

It happened in 1927 only months before Mussolini had crushed what remained of his token political opposition, thus placing his authority beyond question. He was now absolute ruler of Italy and at the zenith of his power.

One day a letter from a chamber-of-commerce official crossed his desk. A young fan of Mussolini's, apparently too shy to communicate directly with the dictator, had spoken with the official and asked if perhaps Il Duce would favor him with a signed photograph. He seemed such a devoted fan, wrote the official, surely Il Duce would grant his humble request.

Any explicit motive for Mussolini's negative response has long since been forgotten, perhaps just his mood on that particular day. What survives for historians to ponder is that chamber-of-commerce memorandum, with a message scrawled across it in the bold letters of Mussolini's own hand: "Request refused."

To soften the tactless refusal, what the young admirer received from a diplomatic secretary was a note that said, "Please thank the above named gentleman for the sentiments that he expresses, but Il Duce was unable to grant his request."

The sharp edge of Mussolini's refusal was thus blunted. Mussolini's admirer received only the diplomatic version of his reply, and the fan remained a fan—as in "fanatic."

For the younger man who worshipped Mussolini from afar, the unknown unwanted enthusiast who had begged for an autographed photograph of Mussolini, continued to follow in Il Duce's footsteps—until one day the two men stood side by side.

The admirer Il Duce ignored in 1927 was Adolf Hitler.

54. Living in Fear

Picture little Al, barely five years old and with a sweet cherubic face.

You've seen the characterizations of adorable English children. The propriety of dress and manners, the aura of defenselessness.

That was little Al right down to the blush on his cheeks and the shine on his tiny shoes. Daddy, a prosperous London importer, called the boy his "little lamb without a spot."

So much for security. Still Daddy, for a reason not yet understood, was intentionally setting up little Al for a blow he never forgot, a blow that became THE REST OF THE STORY.

One day Al was playing around the house, a pretend game of knights and dragons. Daddy was home too that day.

Suddenly Daddy called from upstairs. Little Al ran up to see what Daddy wanted.

Daddy was holding a note in his hand, a note in a sealed envelope. Little Al knew where the police station was, did he not?

Little Al nodded.

Daddy smiled. The boy was to take the note down the street to the police station, hand it to the police chief, and wait for a reply.

Sensing the importance of this message, little Al eagerly accepted the errand. In a flash he was out the door, running through the avenue as fast as his little legs would allow.

By the time he reached the police station he was out of breath, but still beaming with the pride of this new responsibility.

"I'm to wait for an answer," said little Al, thrusting Daddy's message into the police captain's hand.

Reading the note, the police captain grinned at first, then appeared bewildered, then grinned again.

"Come with me," he said.

Little Al followed him through a door, down a long hallway, and through another door—until he and the policeman were standing at the open entrance of a vacant, cold, somber jail cell.

Before little Al knew what was happening or why, he was inside and the iron-barred cell door was clanking shut behind him.

He could hear the police captain's voice trailing away: "This is what we do to naughty boys."

And all was silent.

There was no one to hear little Al's frightened cries for ten minutes or so, a seeming eternity. Then the captain returned, released the boy without explanation, and little Al ran.

For little Al, recalling, the rest of that day is blank.

From that day on he lived a kind of fear. An exceptionally nervous childhood devoid of friends was followed by a lonely adolescence full of trepidations and phobias. A strict Jesuit education, replete with regular corporal punishment, only expanded his vast repertoire of anxieties.

He would approach young manhood with a permanent case of the jitters, with a lump in his throat and a knot in his stomach and a sense of unwarranted suspense.

He was afraid of heights.

He was afraid of what might be lurking around the next corner.

But most of all, and for the most obvious reason, he was and would always be terrified of policemen.

Al never learned, nor has anyone ever attempted to explain, why his father did what he did—what, if anything a little boy might have done to deserve such a fright at the age of five.

Yet, living in fear, Al would one day learn to express fear in a singular manner which would chill us all.

For those ten terror-filled minutes in a London jail inspired a redefinition of theatrical suspense by that boy. He became the motion picture director since described as the master of the involuntary scream: Alfred Hitchcock.

55. Poker Face

World War II, the South Pacific, Green Island.

If you were to round up the Navy officers who served there, and if you were to ask them to recount the losses they endured, the figures they would quote would be American currency.

They lost a great deal of money. And they lost it to a lieutenant named Nick. In poker games.

Nick was the ace poker player of Green Island. His Navy buddies, in mournful retrospect, recall that Nick never lost at poker.

He was unbeatable. And, even more remarkable, before his assignment to Green Island he had never played poker in his life!

The Japanese had evacuated Green Island; our Navy had taken over.

Nick was a ground officer, a lieutenant. His job was to supervise the arrival and distribution of cargo brought by Navy transports.

Despite occasional Japanese bombing raids, there was not a lot of action on Green Island. Unless you count those nightly poker games.

The games were held in a recreation tent with bamboo furnishings and pinup pictures to enliven its otherwise dreary interior.

And remember, Nick had never played poker before. But such was the significance of poker to the Navy men at Green Island that Nick knew he must learn how to play.

Early in his tour of duty he asked a SCAT officer if there were any sure way to win at poker. The officer confessed there was no foolproof technique, but there were many

144

theories; and if Nick had the patience, he, the SCAT officer, would teach him the game.

They played two-handed rounds, no stakes, for four or five days.

Nick's patience was rewarded with a solid knowledge of the basics, and something beyond the basics. It seemed there was a card-playing genius lying dormant in Nick, and that genius soon gained him a reputation throughout the South Pacific.

In the big games under the recreation tent, when the stakes were high, Nick played for keeps.

The losers credited his consistency to his unparalleled "poker face," a splendidly noncommittal expression which remained unvaried before the best and the worst of hands.

With a pair of deuces, he once bluffed a lieutenant commander out of fifteen hundred dollars.

We have forgotten the notorious Navy card shark of Green Island. But we remember the poker face. For Nick didn't spend his considerable wartime winnings, somewhere in the neighborhood of thirty-five hundred dollars. Instead, he invested that money. In himself. In his future.

"Nick" was his Navy nickname. The young lieutenant, remembered by his comrades as the unbeatable poker player who never lost a cent in a game, the poker-wise Navy officer who saved his winnings to invest in a political career, was Richard Nixon.

And now you know THE REST OF THE STORY.

56. On His Own

Othmar Ammann.

He was an engineer for the Port of New York Authority. He wanted out.

Plenty of good years ahead of him; no reason not to quit. So he quit.

Ignoring the risks of leaving a secure job, Othmar Ammann decided he would form his own engineering company. He would open offices around the world. He would fulfill his designer's dreams, would perform architectural miracles.

And he did. Emerging from the comfort of his Port Authority position, he set out on his own.

Because Othmar Ammann was not afraid to take that big step, the world is graced with many magnificent monuments to his memory:

The airport at Addis Ababa, Ethiopia.

Dulles Airport in Washington, D.C.

The Iranian highway system.

The Connecticut and New Jersey turnpikes.

The Pittsburgh, Pennsylvania, Civic Center superstructure.

The U.S. Navy's six-hundred-foot radio telescope.

The Walt Whitman Bridge in Philadelphia.

The Throgs Neck Bridge in New York.

And the world's longest suspension bridge, extending from Staten Island to Brooklyn—the Verrazano-Narrows.

Why designers, architects and engineers are still talking about Othmar Ammann is obvious. But there is more, THE REST OF THE STORY.

Master builder Othmar Ammann was born in Switzerland; he came to the United States at age twenty-five.

He had studied at the Federal Polytechnic Institute in

Zurich, was prepared to take the world of engineering by storm, wound up working for the Port of New York Authority.

His youthful accomplishments had been considerable. Yet would he ever have the freedom to explore the phenomenal reservoir of his intellect while working for someone else?

In 1939, Othmar left his comfortable Port Authority position to form his own engineering company.

You know the rest. He succeeded in his independence. He staggered the students of architectural design with masterpiece after masterpiece. He etched his name in steel and stone across this continent, and then across a grateful globe.

Two of his accomplishments we omitted earlier were New York's George Washington Bridge and San Francisco's Golden Gate Bridge. But then those were completed before his retirement.

We say his *retirement.*

For the true engineering marvels of Othmar Ammann, the accomplishments for which he is most revered by today's engineers, all of the monumental masterworks attesting the genius of Othmar Ammann, were begun and completed between the time he, as a senior citizen, retired at sixty years of age and the time he completed the longest bridge in the world—at eighty-six.

57. The American Kamikazes

Late in 1944, the U.S. Navy at Okinawa suffered some of its heaviest losses of the war.

The reason: new Japanese weapon. Virtually infallible.

Anything we had they could hit, a string of brilliant military successes summed up in one world: *kamikaze*.

The term doesn't specifically refer to suicide. In Japanese, *kamikaze* means "divine wind." A deadly invisible force with a mind of its own.

In graphic terms, the kamikazes were human bombs.

Devastating as were their deeds, just the thought of an elite corps of Japanese pilots flying explosives-laden planes into American ships was awe-inspiring to the Western world.

Morally unconscionable, we said then. And still say. And yet . . . the American Armed Forces had a suicide squadron as well!

The Japanese kamikazes began late in 1944, very late in the war. Our American kamikazes were ready to fly, ready to attack the Japanese, early in 1943. Almost two years before!

During the historic Japanese raid on Pearl Harbor December 7, 1941, for the Japanese, kamikaze suicide tactics were three years in the future.

And yet a month later—sometime in January of 1942—a Pennsylvania surgeon named L. S. Adams arrived in Washington with an idea for one of the most extraordinary military operations ever. A suicide squadron.

Dr. Adams, sidestepping the moral ramifications, offered technological advice only. The upper echelon of the military was apprised, was intrigued.

The proposal found its way to FDR's desk. The President, realizing the effectiveness of such a plan, gave his approval. On direct orders from the White House, Operation X Ray was a reality.

Unlike the airplane-flying Japanese kamikazes of subsequent years, these American kamikazes would be paratroopers with incendiary bombs wired to their chests. Parachuted from bombers high over Japanese cities, the troopers would guide themselves to vulnerable landmarks. The raids would occur in the predawn dark.

"There you have," as one enthusiastic project officer predicted, "the most effective weapon ever dropped from an airplane."

The United States' Kamikaze Corps. In training maneuvers, during one trial run, Operation X Ray proved its devastating potential by accident. At Carlsbad, New Mexico, most of an Army airfield burned to the ground.

Although lives were lost that day, those were apparently the only casualties of Operation X Ray.

In the fall of 1943, after twenty months and two million dollars of preparation, the Army abandoned the operation "solely on the basis of military considerations."

No other official explanation has ever been offered, but it has been suggested the military then learned that an even more deadly instrument of war was about to emerge.

The A-bomb.

So our suicide squadron never made it overseas. But before we turn our attention from the extraordinary secret weapon we almost put to use, there's something you might like to know.

Our American kamikazes were *not* volunteers. They were recruited against their will. Drafted. That is THE REST OF THE STORY.

The recruits who almost died for our cause were ordered into service by the President of the United States. The suicide paratroopers, wired with explosives and bound for Japan—our American kamikazes—were Mexican free-tailed bats.

58. Trist's Tryst

If Nicholas P. Trist sounds like an imagery-ridden name from some forgotten novel, consider the plot.

Nicholas Trist is an affable character with intelligence, polish, general optimism. Such qualities are somewhat incongruous for he is impoverished to the point of near-destitution. He is working as a clerk for the Wilmington and Baltimore Railroad Company in Pennsylvania; after many promotions, the furthest he will go is a position entitled paymaster at a hundred and twelve dollars and fifty cents a month.

It is in the service of the railroad company that Nicholas Trist is to remain for twenty-one years, relegated to the distant memories of his own past prestige.

For once Nicholas P. Trist had it all. He had been a member of the State Department; he had hobnobbed with senators and congressmen, with the President of the United States himself.

Now, as a clerk for the railroad company, he was discarded and forgotten by his former friends in the highest of places, and all because of that one time he disobeyed a direct order from the President.

This has the literary texture of fiction; yet it really happened—to a man named Nicholas P. Trist.

Why his banishment from Washington is THE REST OF THE STORY.

By April 1847, it became apparent that Mexico was willing to make peace with the United States.

President James Polk determined that he should have a peace commissioner with the American Army, someone familiar with the Mexican culture and the Spanish language.

The honor fell upon one Nicholas P. Trist, then chief clerk of the State Department.

With secret orders and a letter signed by the President, emissary Trist set out for Mexico. En route he told the newspapers too much; arriving in Vera Cruz, he told the commanding general of the United States Army too little.

Back home, President Polk was getting nervous.

Shortly after peace negotiations began, Trist sent an unauthorized proposal to Washington. It was his own idea, he said, and he hoped the President liked it.

The President did not like it.

Obviously, Polk's choice for peace commissioner had been a mistake; he sent a letter to Trist saying as much, ordering his emissary to return.

Trist read the letter, then responded with another of his own explaining that he did not want to return. Unprecedented!

As the infuriated President searched for new adjectives by which to denigrate Nicholas Trist, Trist remained in Mexico, negotiated on his own, and on February 2, 1848— again, without any authority to do so—signed a treaty with the Mexicans.

You know the rest . . . that Nicholas P. Trist was thereafter banished from government, that his salary was withheld, that he was forced to take a job with the railroad to feed himself and his family.

But did you know that in spite of it all, the President and the Congress accepted the too-good-to-turn-down treaty which Mr. Trist had designed and signed?

For Nicholas Trist, in direct disobedience to the President of the United States and to the subsequent ruin of his own political career, had chosen to stay in Mexico and to act on his own.

He negotiated for us—U.S.—what is now a fraction of Wyoming and Colorado, and *all* of Arizona, New Mexico, Utah, Nevada and California!

From his determination and his subsequent loss, we won.

59. If We Could Talk to the Animals

Researchers at the University of Oklahoma are realizing Dr. Doolittle's dream: They are "talking to the animals." To one animal in particular—a fifteen-year-old female chimpanzee named Washoe.

This particular research subject was brought from Africa by the U.S. Air Force in 1965. Chimps were being used in the space program at the time, experimentation conducted at Hallomon Air Force Base in New Mexico.

The following year the subject was transported to the University of Nevada for participation in their sign language project. The hypothesis on which these experiments were based: A chimpanzee can be taught to communicate through sign language.

This is not true conceptualization we are talking about. This is basic-recognition communication, mostly single-unit: big, small, up, down . . .

Between 1966 and 1970 the subject, Washoe, learned 130 to 140 signs in the standard American Sign Language system, which is used by the deaf.

Still there was widespread conjecture in the scientific community regarding the significance of this accomplishment. How much could be interpreted as original "expression," and how much, simply, as "monkey see, monkey do"?

Since Pavlov, lower animal forms on the intelligence scale had been shown to be "conditionable"; so were the responses of this particular chimpanzee subject really no more than a conditioned extension of her greater manual dexterity?

Dr. Roger Fouts wanted to find out.

It was he who brought Washoe, the chimp, to the University of Oklahoma Institute of Primate Studies in 1970.

Number one: Catalogue and examine the subject's specific vocabulary and syntax.

Number two: Expand the subject's vocabulary.

Number three: Explore all possibilities of communication, verbal and nonverbal.

Day in, day out. Test after test. And slowly Dr. Fouts learned THE REST OF THE STORY: The subject *was* capable of communication in the human sense—was truly able to conceptualize.

Washoe the chimpanzee was a rational being!

Dr. Fouts and his research team continue to work with Washoe. The University of Oklahoma project has been extended to include other chimpanzees. They are also studying the principles of cultural transmission in action: Washoe the chimp—without human intervention—is now teaching a younger chimpanzee how to talk to people!

Pulitzer Prize winner Dr. Carl Sagan said it: "How smart does a chimpanzee have to be before killing him constitutes murder?" Indeed, how smart would any animal have to be?

At the University of Oklahoma, they are "talking to the animals." And the animals are talking back.

How much do we want to hear from them?

Washoe the chimp is well fed, physically comfortable, safe from harm—and yet since she has learned to express herself in language humans can understand, there is one phrase—a sentence, really—that she "says" more than any other.

Those words, echoing from a lifetime of sterile captivity, the "voice" from the cage: "Let me out!"

60. Armchair Detective

Glasgow, Scotland.

The evening of December 21, 1908.

Cold, misty.

From the lavish Queen's Terrace apartment of Marion Gilchrist, the sounds of violent struggle pour out into the night.

A maid rushes upstairs.

The swarthy, husky figure of a man bolts past her, down the staircase, past the tenant of a neighboring apartment, out onto the street, past a fourteen-year-old girl. Three witnesses.

Miss Marion Gilchrist has been murdered.

Subsequent investigation reveals that a crescent-shaped diamond brooch is missing.

Police scour the pawnshops. A suspect is apprehended: Oscar Slater.

Slater, a German immigrant and owner of a gambling club, had recently been trying to pawn a crescent-shaped diamond brooch.

A search of his apartment uncovers a one-way ticket by ship to New York.

All three witnesses positively identify him.

A speedy trial.

Oscar Slater is sentenced to life imprisonment.

And that would have been that were it not for an "armchair detective." He is THE REST OF THE STORY.

Oscar Slater had been in prison for nineteen years. He was sentenced to life.

Oscar Slater had been forgotten by anybody with cause to care. But Slater knew there was one man outside prison who *should* care. A man with an unquenchable passion for justice. It was to him that the prisoner sent a message: "Please, help me!"

Now this outsider was a physician, a doctor, at best an amateur, an "armchair detective." But Oscar Slater believed in him.

And the doctor, intrigued by the prisoner's letter, began the reexamination of evidence now two decades old.

Oscar Slater had been a gambler, a foreigner. The upstanding Scottish jury might have been prejudiced. Transcripts of the trial showed that the judge himself almost certainly was.

The witnesses. Where were they now? The murdered woman's maid was married and living in America. The fourteen-year-old girl, now thirty-three, still in Scotland. Both were reached. Both admitted to uneasiness over their testimony. Perhaps Slater had not been the man they'd seen after all!

The motive: robbery. An expensive diamond brooch was missing from Marion Gilchrist's apartment. Or had robbery truly been the motive?

The doctor investigated. Some three thousand pounds' worth of jewelry had been left behind in Miss Gilchrist's flat. The theft of the brooch had merely been a cover for someone seeking documents or possibly a will, someone who had known Marion Gilchrist!

Pawnshop records were sought out. Oscar Slater, the convicted murderer, had been trying to pawn his brooch long before Miss Gilchrist's had been stolen!

The doctor was convinced Slater had been innocent.

He petitioned Members of Parliament about the biased manner in which Slater's trial had been conducted. A new inquiry was held. And Oscar Slater, nineteen years in prison, was set free.

But when authorities commended the good doctor on his work and suggested that perhaps he might join in the search for the real murderer, the physician declined. Happy he had had a hand in clearing an innocent man, he was, nonetheless, very busy with his own hobby: writing stories.

The good doctor—the "armchair detective" who took upon himself the real-life role and so set free a man who had been wrongly imprisoned—was Sir Arthur Conan Doyle, the literary creator of the fictional detective Sherlock Holmes!

61. The Old House on the Hill

You are a stranger in these parts, and you've taken a walk into the countryside.

As the brilliant colors of autumn have lured you into wandering, so has your mind been dazzled into forgetfulness. Your way being momentarily lost, you look up and about you. And there, atop a high hill, is a huge old house.

Let's walk up there for a closer look.

As the dry leaves rustle in your path the old house looms larger before you. There is no sign of activity from without or within. Tall windows, tall columns, tall chimneys. A lonely feeling.

Obviously uninhabited, equally obviously uninhabitable. The place is a ruin, somber, desolate. Vegetation has grown up all around; the windows are broken.

It's getting late now; you ought really to turn back. But curiosity is getting the better of you. As you expected, the big door on the west side is not only open—it's practically falling off its hinges.

Now you're in the main hall. There is a large horseshoe-shaped second-story balcony with no apparent staircase leading to it. What a grand home this must have been once upon a time!

Your pensiveness is broken by sudden sounds. Was that a moan you heard? And then some sort of dragging or grinding from below?

Once more your curiosity has overcome other considerations and you set off to search for the source of the sounds. Your search ends in the basement. For some reason, livestock have been allowed to take shelter here. Cattle. Now you've seen everything! And one by one, the questions come.

How could such a place, surely once so lovely, have been neglected and consigned to decay?

Doesn't anyone know it's here?

I'll tell you this much: The original owner, impoverished before his death, sought permission from the authorities to raffle off his home. It, and everything in it, went for a song, and eventually the old house was abandoned.

And I'll tell you something else, THE REST OF THE STORY.

You, right now, are carrying a picture of the old house in your pocket! And the countryside walk you took a hundred years ago.

In 1879, the old house on the hill looked precisely as you saw it. Grain was sometimes milled and stored on the parquet floors of the drawing room. The basement had become a cattle barn.

In 1862, the house was bequeathed to the American people, and Congress turned it down. Congress, preoccupied with the Civil War, had no time for petty real estate.

For twenty years the home declined toward total collapse even though its designer, its builder, its original owner—was also the designer and author of our Declaration of Independence.

The old house on the hill, restored at last from ruin and with us still—the same house on the tail of your nickel—was the home of Thomas Jefferson. Monticello.

62. Paderewski Smiled

Anyone who had heard the young boy's playing might have told you he would be a great concert pianist someday.

Not only was he remarkably talented, but he possessed even at seven the self-discipline that makes a great musician. Before the keyboard at five each morning, he practiced passionately for many hours a day. Lessons, twice a week.

In the beginning he had studied piano with a next-door neighbor lady and in a short while he was playing better than she. Now he was studying with Mrs. E. C. White, renowned pianist and teacher, protégé of Theodor Leschetitzky. Leschetitzky, incidentally, was the incomparable European master who had taught Josef Lhévinne and Paderewski.

It was a considerable musical tradition to which this youngster was an heir. With each day he reinforced everyone's high hopes for his future.

The tiny hands became larger, the fingers longer and stronger. In his early teens no technical exercise was beyond his grasp, few masterworks of Bach, Beethoven or Liszt beyond his comprehension.

It was in 1900 that Mrs. White surprised her star pupil with the news that the great Paderewski was coming to town. She, Mrs. White, would take the boy to the concert.

For a budding pianist of fifteen, there could have been no greater delight. He would actually hear Paderewski play. Not on the phonograph, as he was accustomed to hearing him, but in person!

Sleepless nights spanned the announcement and the evening of the event. At the appointed hour, Mrs. White and her young protégé joined the eager throng and passed through the auditorium doors.

As the last audience member was seated, the houselights dimmed and the imposing figure of that era's most celebrated pianist strode onstage.

With the opening bars, the youngster sat wide-eyed. Time lapsed into timelessness. A crushing pain in the boy's chest; enraptured, he had forgotten to breathe.

When at last the staggering event was finished and the music was no more, the youngster, still dazed, heaved a sigh.

That is what he wanted to be. The greatest pianist in the whole wide world.

Then Mrs. White nudged him. "You haven't seen the last of Mr. Paderewski," she said.

She would take the boy backstage to meet him.

Even as his teacher spoke, the boy began to tremble. This wasn't happening, was it? Yes, it was. Minutes later, the two were standing at a dressing-room door—and pianist Paderewski emerged to greet them, wringing his magnificent hands with a white handkerchief.

He and Mrs. White exchanged fond memories of their teacher, Leschetitzky. Then his attention turned to the boy.

"A gifted young pianist," said Mrs. White.

"Indeed," said Paderewski.

The boy spoke, still trembling. He had studied Mr. Paderewski's own Minuet. But there was a passage, the proper execution of which he was uncertain.

His hand at the boy's shoulder, Paderewski walked back to the empty stage and to the piano. It was all right, the master assured him, there was no one else in the hall. Would the young man please demonstrate what he meant?

The boy sat down before the long grand piano, and he played. Paderewski, lifting his eyes to Mrs. White, smiled.

Proud Mrs. White, her own eyes moist and glistening, knew what the smile meant.

Approval.

For most all the days of his years she had guided this obviously gifted fledgling—and now he was taking to the sky.

Surely he would become a great artist.

Whether Mrs. White's prediction would have come true, no one can say. The course of this young man's life was to be changed for him.

The very next year, his father lost everything in the Kansas City grain market. He, the boy, would have to go to work—and so his dreams of the concert stage were done.

In later years he would neglect his musical talent and speak of it only lightly. Those who had known him as a boy knew better.

For the gifted youngster who rose each day at five to practice, the talented interpreter of masterworks before his teens, the accomplished musician who had won the greatest prize a pianist of his generation could hope for, Paderewski's smile, was destined for greatness of another kind.

You remember this boy pianist for the man of destiny he became: Harry S. Truman.

Only now you know THE REST OF THE STORY.

63. MacCarthy Era

It has been called the MacCarthy Era.

The big war was over. An entire nation breathed a sigh of relief. A new mission was at hand, under the banner of conservatism. It seemed that the people, though weary of bloodshed, were not yet weary of war.

The new, illusive enemy was liberalism. The conflict, ideological.

Although most chose sides and although many took up arms, history tells us that the conservative banner was lofted the highest by one man. Some called him a saint, others, a devil. His name, Joseph MacCarthy.

In the calm of retrospect, we review his era; we see him as the reflected image of a nation seeking stability. Many would still contend that his crusade was justified, that his cause, though now outdated, served its purpose in its time.

Among his enemies, some forgave. Others never forgot.

But the world has yet to recognize THE REST OF THE STORY.

It has been called the MacCarthy Era perhaps incorrectly. For it was a period in the history of a great country that, for better or worse, belonged to everyone.

Contrary to popular suspicion, Joseph MacCarthy did not create a climate of retribution against liberalism.

It was already there! Even before his rise to prominence, a nation of people sorely feared the enemy in their midst, sought desperately for a spokesman in government. Joseph MacCarthy was that voice.

Ostensibly his crusade was sanctioned by the highest authority in the land, although public reinforcement of this sanction was never necessary.

With increased authority and rapidly mounting popular

support, Joseph MacCarthy set out to do battle with those who would dismantle the old order.

From his seat in government, he named names. Many of those, prestigious ones, lost their prestige, never to regain it.

With the same bulldog tenacity he had demonstrated during the war, Joseph MacCarthy clung to this new cause.

He attacked the unrestricted freedom of the press which had made him a hero; the press was potentially a tool of evil, he said, undeniably subversive.

And in the MacCarthy Era, it seemed that subversives were everywhere.

In the progress of the continuing "witch-hunt," a high-ranking officer in the nation's own military was disgraced. At last, when Joseph MacCarthy's crusade of conservatism came to an end, his enemies vowed that it would never happen again.

But it did happen again. Thousands of miles away and a century and a half later . . . it happened all over again.

In America.

For the ideologically torn nation we've been describing was France. The era, the early nineteenth century.

The highest authority in the land, who delegated the dirty work to someone else, was King Louis XVIII. The liberal-baiting government-based crusader was Count Robert Joseph MacCarthy.

And France survived.

64. Helping Hand

This next is closed-circuit to the staff nurse at Peninsula Hospital in Redwood City, California. Nurse, you claim you saw attendants wheel a twelve-foot, three-hundred-pound bottlenose dolphin into emergency last year.

You were right!

Of all the aquatic performers at Redwood City's Marine World, perhaps none is more talented nor better loved than a dolphin named Mr. Spock.

On Thursday, February 23, 1978, Mr. Spock was off duty, playfully swimming about in his tank.

Midafternoon, a Marine World diver plunged in with him to repair a fallen pipe which was a part of the tank's filtration system.

Mr. Spock was swimming around while the diver was in the tank, working on the pipe. The diver, preparing to remount the pipe bracket, temporarily slipped one of the three-inch stainless steel lag screws into the bracket hole; he hesitated to retrieve a tool, and when he looked back . . . the steel screw was gone.

The diver looked everywhere in the tank; the hardware—was nowhere.

Mr. Spock had swiped and swallowed the huge, sharp screw! Immediately the Marine World veterinary clinic was notified; Mr. Spock was lifted from his tank, taken to the operating table.

An operation was *not* suggested; that measure would be too drastic.

Mr. Spock was *not* to be tranquilized; that could kill him. But a dolphin can live out of water for up to twenty-four hours, so Mr. Spock up to then was all right.

The pressure was on Marine World's veterinary technician. He tried to induce vomiting.

That didn't work. "Are you *sure* he swallowed the screw?" the veterinarian asked.

They had to be sure. So they took Mr. Spock to Peninsula Hospital, a people hospital, for X rays. If the sharp-pointed razor-threaded screw was inside Mr. Spock, he was in trouble.

And the X rays confirmed he was in trouble.

But there was some good news: the screw was in the first of Mr. Spock's three stomachs; technically, the offending object was accessible through the dolphin's throat.

A staff physician at Peninsula Hospital, Dr. Roost, agreed to probe Mr. Spock's gullet with his fiber-optics equipment. There was also a gizmo on the end of this probe with which Dr. Roost could snag the screw if he could see it.

But the stainless steel screw, obscured by a recently eaten fish, could not be seen through Dr. Roost's equipment.

Four hours after Mr. Spock was removed from his tank, he was back.

There was an all-night vigil. At daybreak, Marine World president Mike Demetrios and his staff veterinarian were still contemplating the plight of Mr. Spock.

The veterinarian remarked that if his arm were just nine inches longer—just *nine inches*—he could reach down Mr. Spock's throat and retrieve the screw.

That's when Mike Demetrios remembered Cliff.

Once more, Mr. Spock was pulled from his tank, taken to the Marine World clinic. Cliff was rushed to the scene.

And Cliff, thoroughly informed and scrubbed, under the precise supervision of the veterinarian, slowly, carefully, reached all the way into Mr. Spock's stomach.

Mission accomplished.

Today, Mr. Spock is back at play, healthy in every way, thanks to Cliff.

Oh, Cliff is Clifford Ray. The center on the Golden State Warriors basketball team.

He is six feet nine.

His helping hand was on the end of an arm almost four feet long!

And now you know THE REST OF THE STORY.

65. Knowing by Heart

The evening of June 25, 1886, in Rio de Janeiro: the Brazilians versus the Italians, and the Italians were losing.

Not a war with guns.

Not a sporting event.

An opera.

The brawl had begun in the hall even before the curtain had risen—and on both sides of the curtain. Total confusion. Shrieking, stamping, whistling, jeering.

Just what pushed these ordinarily sensible artists and operagoers to the brink of physical violence is THE REST OF THE STORY . . .

First, the performers.

A touring Italian opera company organized by impresario Carlo Rossi.

Since this was to be a tour of Brazil, Signor Rossi, minding his diplomacy, was careful to choose a Brazilian as chief conductor. Leopoldo Miguez was his name.

Naturally, most of the opera singers, as well as the first-chair orchestra members and the chorus master and the assistant conductor—were Italian. An Italian opera company. So there they were in Brazil, mostly Italian performers with a Brazilian star conductor.

Their first performance in Rio was the opera *Faust*.

The next day's newspaper reviews were scathing.

No one in the touring company was happy.

The Italian performers blamed their Brazilian conductor, calling him personally overbearing and musically incompetent.

Simultaneously, the Brazilian conductor sent an open letter to the newspapers. The performance had been sabotaged by the "foreigners" in the company, it said. The "foreigners," meaning the Italians. The conductor's letter further stated that he was withdrawing from the company.

That brings us to June 25.

The scheduled opera, *Aida*.

Everyone in the audience has read the published complaint of their hometown conductor.

Not only had the Italians insulted him, they reasoned, but in doing so they had offended all of Brazil.

What we have here is the making of a war.

The operagoers, the culture crowd—ordinarily polite, sedate—have blood in their eyes.

The assistant conductor, whose job it is to carry on, steps to the podium in the orchestra pit.

There is a rustling of programs as the audience searches for his name in print. Assistant conductor: Superti.

An Italian!

Before Superti can raise his baton, a wave of jeers and whistles washes over him.

Superti storms from the pit.

Now it's impresario Rossi's turn. Planning to smooth the ruffled feathers with a kind word or two, he strides before the lowered curtain.

Rossi! Another Italian!

And he too is drowned out, chased away.

Backstage is humming, and not musically. Who's left to take over?

Moments later the chorus master edges his way toward the podium.

The whispered word travels like wildfire through the audience. Chorus master, chorus master . . .

Another rustling of programs.

Chorus master: Venturi.

Yet another Italian!

An explosion of stomping and hooting. Good-bye Venturi.

Backstage once more, singers are weeping, impresario Rossi is pacing. If this concert is canceled, the entire tour may be also. That would leave a lot of folks with no money, and on the wrong side of the Atlantic to suit them.

Meanwhile, back in the pit, one of the musicians stands, points, yells out, "What about him? Let him try! He knows the opera by heart!"

The object of this sudden outburst is a nineteen-year-old cellist buried back in the section.

A nobody.

That he had, at the tour's outset, been rather casually designated assistant chorus master is hardly a recommendation in and of itself.

But this is no time for credentials.

In seconds he is being swarmed by the desperate opera cast. If not he, then who will bail them out?

Elbowing his way through the confusion, impresario Rossi approaches the bewildered young man. Even at a distance, the message is clear: Get out to that podium and do something—*anything*.

The back-row cellist obeys.

As he rises before the conductor's desk the audience is distracted from its turbulence. Who's this now? A cello player, someone says. An Italian? Who knows? He's not listed in the program. He might even be—Brazilian!

The musician who had singled him out was right about one thing: he, the young man, *does* know the opera by heart.

So much the better.

With a flourish, the slender dark-eyed youth closes the score in front of him.

What's this? By memory?

And as the strings begin the opening bars of *Aida*, pianissimo, a real-life legend is born.

The young man—the obscure cellist who rose to the occasion, making it and himself a success—was almost not there that night.

He had planned to play hooky from that particular performance; buried in the cellos he would not have been missed.

Instead, he was besieged by his conscience, his musician's sense of duty. And because he was—because he showed up for the performance that evening—he awakened the next morning to critical acclaim, and to his new post as chief conductor for the remainder of the tour.

It was only after the opera had finished that the audience learned: he, too, was Italian.

But by then, in the wake of a splendid performance, it made little difference.

Time alone would tell that the slender nineteen-year-old with the deep, dark, penetrating eyes—the obscure cellist who almost missed the opportunity of a lifetime—was destined to be hailed as the greatest conductor who ever lived.

Arturo Toscanini.

66. Mirror
in the Ocean

On August 4, 1914, the magnificent British luxury liner *Carmania* was three days out of New York Harbor and on her way to Liverpool with eight hundred passengers.

Shortly before midnight that night she was approached by a British cruiser flashing this message in light signals:

CARMANIA—WAR IS DECLARED—DARKEN SHIP—RADIO SILENCE.

These precautions were taken. The *Carmania* arrived in Liverpool at 8:00 A.M., August 7. At once the British Admiralty assumed command; she, the *Carmania*, now in service of the Royal Navy, would be converted into a warship.

The conversion process was swift, efficient: 4.7-caliber guns were installed; range: 9300 yards.

By Friday, August 14—only a week after she had entered port as a first-class Atlantic liner—the *Carmania* was at sea again, but now as a fully equipped armed cruiser.

Her refrigerated stocks, originally intended for the passengers' meals, had been left on board. That included the best salmon and sole and beef and eggs and fresh fruit and grouse—so officers and crew ate well.

Docking in the West Indies, September 2, the *Carmania* was promptly loaded with coal and wartime provisions. At 10:00 A.M. on the eleventh she received her orders: Scout the vicinity of Trinidad Island for enemy ships.

Three days later at 9:30 in the morning the *Carmania*'s masthead lookout sighted the island. One hour and thirty-four minutes passed. Another sighting: a ship off the coast of Trinidad.

171

At that point the *Carmania* might as well have sailed into the Twilight Zone. That ship in the distance—the vessel seen from the decks of the *Carmania*—was the *Carmania*! Or at least a ship that bore her name and looked exactly like her.

The other vessel was in fact a German liner, also converted into a warship; a German luxury liner, the *Cap Trafalgar*, which had been disguised in every outward detail as the *Carmania*.

Considering the short-range guns which had been installed on the German ship, she could be effective in battle only if she could get close enough to the enemy.

Made to look like the British liner *Carmania*, she, the German ship, could achieve this goal.

Yet no one aboard the *Cap Trafalgar* might have predicted a coincidental mid-Atlantic meeting with the real *Carmania*, and that was the German ship's downfall.

On September 14 the disguised *Cap Trafalgar* was attacked, crippled and sunk by the real *Carmania*.

But that's not THE REST OF THE STORY.

You see, that mirror in the ocean—encountered in disbelief by the *Carmania*—was a two-way mirror.

Just as the *Cap Trafalgar* was redesigned—even to the dismantling of one funnel—to look like the *Carmania*, the *Carmania* was also redesigned and repainted so that she could get closer to the enemy. In the process a dummy funnel was added to the British ship.

That's right.

When the two vessels met in mid-Atlantic, September 14, 1914, each by coincidence was disguised in detail as the other! With two oceans to get lost in they had somehow found each other! That is THE REST OF THE STORY.

67. The War Machine

To his classmates at West Point, he was "Old Jack." To General Robert E. Lee, he was "my trusty right arm." To his troops he was "Old Blue Light" until the first battle of Bull Run. Then one of the Confederate soldiers observed that their commander, standing bravely in the heat of the fray, looked very much . . . like a stone wall.

That was General Thomas J. Jackson. "Stonewall" Jackson.

In the War Between the States, his brigade—the First Brigade—was perhaps the Confederacy's most devastating war machine.

He trained his men to precision; he conditioned them to the height of responsiveness; he transformed their numbers into a cohesive organism, a virtually unconquerable instrument of war.

For the men who served under "Stonewall" Jackson, obedience was a key concept, discipline a way of life. Still, the General loved his men, and the men loved their General.

The images of the leader and the led blurred, fused. "Stonewall" Jackson and the First Brigade became an unbeatable package deal, the dread of the Union Army.

Of all the military units in the South, his was the killing machine.

It is for this reason that I wish to focus your attention on "Stonewall" Jackson's last battle, a fight both won and lost. That is THE REST OF THE STORY.

During the Civil War, the secret weapon of the Confederacy was no secret.

It was General "Stonewall" Jackson and his First Brigade. The discipline, the unflinching obedience of Jackson's men, the military brilliance of their leader, combined to comprise a most remarkable war machine. The tactical efficiency and ingenuity of Jackson's last battle was so outstanding that most modern military textbooks include a description of it.

It took place in May 1863, an encounter with Union general Joseph Hooker near Chancellorsville, Virginia.

I won't diminish the intricacy of Jackson's maneuvers by attempting to synopsize them here; but in the end, after already having divided his troops, Jackson divided them again, swung around to the right in a surprise attack and extended himself and his division beyond his own lines. They routed the enemy.

The battle had been won. And then, a tragedy for the Confederates. General "Stonewall" Jackson, returning from the attack, was shot three times.

The wounds in themselves were not fatal. Jackson lived for several days in a weakened condition and then died of pneumonia.

Considering the morale of his men to the last, he had requested that his wounds be kept secret.

But the troops knew all along.

Among the strict orders he had issued to his brigade before the battle was immediately to gun down any unknown soldiers, and to ask questions later.

That is why Jackson's men, ever obedient, conditioned to react quickly, responded to the rustling in the dense woods of Chancellorsville by opening fire.

The "unknown soldier" they felled was their own General, "Stonewall" Jackson, returning from that daring foray beyond his own lines!

In the end, the unstoppable First Brigade—the Confederacy's most magnificent killing machine—had not broken down, but had merely turned on itself.

68. Twelve
to the Bar

This is a test. Not an easy test.

You are about to read the names of twelve of our nation's most prominent lawyers. Only one of them was a law school dropout.

Can you guess his name?

Ready . . . get set . . .

Patrick Henry. Member of the Continental Congress, governor of Virginia. He passed his oral bar examinations in 1760; within three years he had handled more than eleven hundred cases.

John Jay. He was admitted to the bar in 1768, subsequently distinguishing himself as the first Chief Justice of the Supreme Court.

John Marshall. Another Supreme Court Chief Justice; he passed his bar exams in 1780.

William Wirt. Barely twenty, he practiced law in Culpeper County, Virginia, eventually becoming United States Attorney General.

Now remember, one of these nationally prominent lawyers was a law school dropout, and you're trying to discover him . . .

Roger Taney. Admitted to practice in 1799, he worked his way up. First Secretary of the Treasury, then Chief Justice of the Supreme Court.

Daniel Webster. He was admitted to the Boston bar in 1805, established a phenomenal legal reputation; subsequently he was appointed Secretary of State in 1841.

Salmon Chase. United States Senator, Chief Justice of the Supreme Court, he gained his early prominence as a defense attorney for runaway slaves.

Abraham Lincoln. Sixteenth president of the United States, an occupation greatly enhanced by his former experience as a lawyer.

Stephen Douglas. Admitted to the bar in 1834, he later became representative, then senator, from Illinois. He debated Lincoln.

Clarence Darrow. A lawyer of world renown, his most famous case was the Scopes, so-called Monkey, trial of 1925.

Robert Storey. Born in 1893, he was president of the American Bar Association in 1952 and 1953.

Strom Thurmond. Admitted to the bar in 1930, he later became governor of South Carolina, then senator from that state.

Those are the twelve.

Only *one* of them abandoned law school after the first year, never to return.

Once more, names only:

Patrick Henry . . .

John Jay . . .

John Marshall . . .

William Wirt . . .

Roger Taney . . .

Daniel Webster . . .

Salmon Chase . . .

Abraham Lincoln . . .

Stephen Douglas . . .

Clarence Darrow . . .

Robert Storey . . .

Strom Thurmond . . .

Time's up. Of the names you've just read, only one was a law school dropout. He was Clarence Darrow.

That's right. Clarence Darrow, the one name the whole world associates with the practice of law, attended law school for one year only. He did not distinguish himself and dropped out to study law on his own.

Oh, did I mention that the other eleven—those eleven most distinguished American lawyers—could *not* have dropped out of law school, because they never went to law school at all? That is THE REST OF THE STORY.

69. Sir Jeffery's Peril

In the court of King Charles I the most remarkable knight of all was Sir Jeffery Hudson.

Immortalized in the art and literature of the seventeenth century, Sir Jeffery was no mere legend. His deeds of valor, his swashbuckling life of romance and adventure, are a matter of record.

Of all his perils, however, there was one adventure in particular from which Sir Jeffery narrowly escaped with his life. While he had easily survived the fields of battle and the fields of honor and even the jealous husbands, one day in a very unswashbuckling way Sir Jeffery nearly drowned.

From an early age, Jeffery Hudson was destined to curry royal favor.

At nine he was taken into the service of the Duke and Duchess of Buckingham. There he was trained, later to be presented to the King and Queen of England.

Jeffery's first royal post was at Hampton Court on the Thames. When he was eleven years old, he was accepted into the British diplomatic service.

His first mission involved a trip to France, the return voyage of which was interrupted by Flemish pirates off the coast of Dunkirk. The gallantry he demonstrated throughout this predicament would typify him in later years: a lifetime of adventure was just beginning.

Still in his teens, he sailed for Holland with the earls of Warwick and Northampton to aid the Dutch in their war for independence against the Spaniards.

By 1637 reports of Jeffery's valor reached England and, a year later, at the age of nineteen, Jeffery was greeted in his homeland as a hero.

He was knighted *Sir* Jeffery Hudson. The ladies of the royal court fought for his attention. A book was written about him, and ever after each year of his life was a match for the one preceding.

As a captain in the King's army, Sir Jeffery fought bravely against the Puritans who sought to overthrow Charles I. When the royal cause was lost, he escaped with the Queen to France.

From that time until the day he died he experienced an incredible succession of romantic exploits, duels to the death, unjust imprisonment and escape, world travel and battles with pirates and slavery among the Turks.

At thirty-nine, he returned to England to the friendly court of Charles II.

For seven years he maintained his reputation as a gallant knight and ladies' man before retiring to the quiet life of a country squire.

But retirement, though pleasant, was not sufficient to satisfy the adventurous spirit of Sir Jeffery Hudson. In 1679, at the age of sixty, he emerged from the comfort of his country home and his pension to join the secret service of the King.

How is it that Sir Jeffery's greatest peril, his closest brush with death, was a near drowning? And that near drowning happened one day when Sir Jeffery went to wash his hands and face . . . and nearly drowned in the washbasin!

The reason is found best in the silence of those remnants which survive him in the portraits of Sir Jeffery and the Queen which hang today in Hampton Court, and in his clothing, which has been preserved in the Ashmolean Museum at Oxford.

For the gallant Sir Jeffery Hudson, the knight whose days were laced with heroism and romantic intrigue, the remarkable cavalier, the valiant warrior, the notorious lover, Sir Jeffery Hudson, in his stocking feet . . . was only eighteen inches tall!

That is THE REST OF THE STORY.

70. Off the Wall

In 1899 four newspaper reporters from Denver, Colorado, set out to tear down the Great Wall of China. They almost succeeded. Literally.

The four met by chance one Saturday night, in a Denver railway depot. Al Stevens, Jack Tournay, John Lewis, Hal Wilshire. They represented the four Denver papers: the *Post*, the *Times*, the *Republican*, the *Rocky Mountain News*.

Each had been sent by his respective newspaper to dig up a story—*any* story—for the Sunday editions; so the reporters were in the railroad station, hoping to snag a visiting celebrity should one happen to arrive that evening by train.

None arrived that evening, by train or otherwise. The reporters started commiserating. For them, no news was bad news; all were facing emptyhanded return trips to their city desks.

Al declared he was going to make up a story and hand it in. The other three laughed.

Someone suggested they all walk over to the Oxford Hotel and have a beer. They did.

Jack said he liked Al's idea about faking a story. Why didn't each of them fake a story and get off the hook?

John said Jack was thinking too small. Four half-baked fakes didn't cut it. What they needed was one real whopper they could all use.

Another round of beers.

A phony domestic story would be too easy to check on, so they began discussing foreign angles that would be difficult to verify. And that is THE REST OF THE STORY.

China was distant enough, it was agreed. They would write about China.

John leaned forward, gesturing dramatically in the dim light of the barroom. Try *this* one on, he said: Group of American engineers, stopping over in Denver en route to China. The Chinese government is making plans to demolish the Great Wall; our engineers are bidding on the job.

Harold was skeptical. Why would the Chinese want to destroy the Great Wall of China?

John thought for a moment. They're tearing down the ancient boundary to symbolize international goodwill, to welcome foreign trade!

Another round of beers.

By 11:00 P.M. the four reporters had worked out the details of their preposterous story. After leaving the Oxford Bar, they would go over to the Windsor Hotel. They would sign four fictitious names to the hotel register. They would instruct the desk clerk to tell anyone who asked that four New Yorkers had arrived that evening, had been interviewed by reporters, had left early the next morning for California.

The Denver newspapers carried the story. All four of them. Front page.

In fact, the *Times* headline that Sunday read: GREAT CHINESE WALL DOOMED! PEKING SEEKS WORLD TRADE!

Of course, the story was a phony, a ludicrous fabrication concocted by four capricious newsmen in a hotel bar.

But their story was taken seriously, was picked up and expanded by newspapers in the Eastern U.S. and then by newspapers abroad.

When the Chinese themselves learned that the Americans were sending a demolition crew to tear down their national monument, most were indignant; some were enraged.

Particularly incensed were the members of a secret society, a volatile group of Chinese patriots who were already wary of foreign intervention.

They, inspired by the story, exploded, rampaged against the foreign embassies in Peking, slaughtered hundreds of missionaries.

In two months, twelve thousand troops from six countries joined forces, invaded China with the purpose of protecting their own countrymen.

The bloodshed which followed, sparked by a journalistic hoax invented in a barroom in Denver, became the white-hot international conflagration known to every high school history student . . . as the Boxer Rebellion.

71. The Gianinnis

Her name is Doris Gianinni. Gianinni is her maiden name. She is proud of her Italian ancestry, especially proud of how it relates to our American history.

Doris's family, five generations before, had been brought to this country at the behest of Thomas Jefferson.

Their home in the Old World was a little Italian town called Lucca. The Gianinnis were growers of fruit trees and vines, tenders of vineyards, makers of wine.

About 1773, three years before our country was a country, the Gianinni family received a communication from America from a fellow countryman who had emigrated there some years before.

His name was Philip Mazzei. Philip had only recently befriended revolutionary statesman Thomas Jefferson. Their common interest was horticulture.

Mazzei and Jefferson discussed the feasibility of forming an agricultural company because Jefferson was fascinated by the prospect of growing exotic trees and vines in America. Mazzei told Jefferson that they would need Italian laborers for the project.

That's when the Gianinnis entered the scene. Philip Mazzei, at Jefferson's request, prepared to take over land adjoining Jefferson's Virginia estate.

"Come to America," Mazzei wrote the Gianinnis. "Let us accept this glorious challenge."

The Gianinnis did come to America, worked with Mazzei and Jefferson. The project lasted about four years, through the autumn of 1778.

Although the horticultural experiment suffered and eventually failed in the Virginia climate, Thomas Jefferson—through his association with Mazzei and the Gianinnis—gained a deep affinity for all things Mediterranean.

183

Historians recall that Jefferson favored friendship and trade between the United States and the Mediterranean countries, that he was particularly in awe of Italian agricultural skill and artistic heritage.

Jefferson's respect is one reason Doris Gianinni is so proud of her family. For after the Virginia experiment failed, Doris's ancestors stayed in Virginia.

Now Doris represents a sixth generation of Gianinnis in America. And *her* son is THE REST OF THE STORY.

He became a writer; because of something he wrote, we know his mother, Doris Gianinni.

We don't know her by that name nor did we know previously about her Italian ancestry.

For nine years, however, she has been portrayed in the setting her son remembers, in the mountains of Virginia. Her writer son is Earl Hamner.

Earl's mother, whose Italian forefathers worked alongside Thomas Jefferson—Doris Gianinni we know as Olivia Walton.

72. A Question
of Bravery

In April 1936, FBI director J. Edgar Hoover was called
to testify before a Senate committee.

The courage of one of the Bureau's men was indirectly
impugned; the G-man in question, during his years of
service, had never made an arrest.

Director Hoover did not like cowards. And for the
United States Senate to question the bravery of *any* Bureau
agent was a reflection on the entire agency.

To ignore the implication would be a blot on the Bureau.

So the Director elected instead to send the agent whose
courage had been impugned—to send that fellow on the
next most dangerous mission, wherever it occurred.

He did not have long to wait.

It was to be an historic confrontation—with the nation's
most cold-blooded killer, the successor to John Dillinger:
Alvin Karpis, Public Enemy Number One.

That was the hood this FBI man would have to capture.

The badman's whereabouts were learned. New Orleans.
A small apartment building a half mile from the business
district.

May 1. The dead of night. FBI men surrounded the
apartment, waited. And leading the squad, taking the heat,
out in front where the first bullets might fly, was the G-man
whose courage had been publicly questioned only two
weeks before.

Karpis and two other gang members, unaware of their
surveillance, emerged from the building, headed for their
car.

"Halt! FBI!"

But neither Karpis nor the others moved for a gun, nor

tried to run. They froze. In fact, Karpis himself, who had once boasted that he would never be taken alive, was most frightened of all!

Said the agent in charge of the capture, the FBI man who had never before made an arrest:

"We took him without firing a shot. That marked him as a dirty yellow rat. He was scared to death when we closed in on him. He shook all over—his voice, his hands, his knees."

The apprehension of Alvin Karpis—in both senses of the word—made front pages coast to coast. One G-man in particular was hailed as a hero. And from that day on, no one —neither the public nor the Senate nor FBI director Hoover himself—ever questioned that agent's bravery.

A week later, this same G-man went to Toledo and captured Harry Campbell, a Karpis accomplice. And when at last the agent returned to Washington, it was concluded that he had proved himself; he could get back to his desk where he belonged.

Director Hoover could not have been happier, nor more proud.

And with good reason . . .

For the forty-one-year-old FBI man whose courage was in question and whose test was comprised of two dangerous missions—was himself the director of the Federal Bureau of Investigation, J. Edgar Hoover.

And now you know THE REST OF THE STORY.

73. Orenthal

San Francisco's Potrero Hill is still a poor South City neighborhood. In 1947 it was a real ghetto.

Nineteen forty-seven. That was the year Orenthal was born.

Orenthal was the boy's name, yet that was the least of his problems.

Orenthal was deformed. Rickets is a poverty-related disease, related to malnutrition. And that's just what Orenthal had, rickets. His vitamin- and mineral-deficient diet softened his bones, made them weak. His legs began to bow under the weight of his body.

Too poor to afford braces, Orenthal's mother rigged up a homemade contraption. Attempting to correct the pigeon-toed, bowlegged condition, she reversed her son's shoes: right shoe on the left foot, and the opposite. Then there was an improvised metal bar across the shoe tops, to keep the feet pointing straight ahead.

Orenthal survived the rickets and the rack. By six his bones had hardened, his legs were permanently bowed, his calves were as spindly as soda straws, and his head was disproportionately large.

Nicknames from the neighborhood children? Oh, yes! "Pencil-Legs" . . . and "Waterhead." Eventually Orenthal, whose real name wasn't much better, compensated for those things wherein fate had shortchanged him by acting tough.

There were a half dozen street gangs on Potrero Hill: the Gladiators, the Sheiks, the Roman Gents, the Persian Warriors. At thirteen, Orenthal became president of the Gladiators. For all the fighting, he was arrested only three times; that was the crowning achievement of his early youth.

187

How to succeed at anything with two malformed legs, an outsized head, a juvenile arrest record and a name like Orenthal . . . is THE REST OF THE STORY.

His legs are still bowed from childhood rickets. His head is still large in proportion to his body. The memories of his mother bailing him out of the slammer at midnight are still vivid. His name is still Orenthal. Yet today he is a fine and refined, remarkably successful gentle man.

He lives in the exclusive Brentwood district of Los Angeles. He drives a Rolls-Royce.

His office, not far from his home, is located in a bank building. It is furnished against tones of brown and rust in wood and suede.

Orenthal is a busy executive with his own production company. He handles personally most of his finances, most of his business negotiations.

He has contracts with the American and National Broadcasting Companies and with other firms and agencies. He's there, he's made it, in the same world which once seemed so intimidating.

Oh, the ghetto is not forgotten. Nor is the diet-deficiency disease he later called polio to avoid the stigma of poverty. Nor has success clouded the memories of nicknames like "Pencil-Legs" and "Waterhead."

Nor has he come so far from the streets that he cannot recite the names of the guys in the gangs.

Orenthal does not have to act tough anymore. He is tough. Tough enough to be gentle.

The deformity of his legs is with him forever to remind him of all that has passed, to heighten the gratitude for all he now has.

The home in Brentwood, the Rolls, the many successful careers. Including football.

The plush office with his name on the door belongs to Orenthal James Simpson.

O. J. Simpson.

74. The Nothing Something

Captain Hanson Gregory was in command of his own vessel at the age of nineteen. He was one of the youngest sea captains ever to sail from the coast of Maine.

For saving the lives of an entire shipwrecked Spanish crew Captain Gregory, still nineteen, was decorated by Spain's Queen Isabella.

But that's not why Hanson Gregory is remembered. We know him because he invented—absolutely nothing!

Confusing? Not after THE REST OF THE STORY.

Two decades after the death of Captain Hanson Gregory, a furious debate, sponsored by a national organization, was held at New York's Astor Hotel.

It was late in November 1941. The judges were Clifton Fadiman, Franklin P. Adams, Elsa Maxwell. Leaders of the opposing sides were Fred E. Crockett of Camden, Maine, and attorney Henry A. Ellis of Cape Cod, Massachusetts.

The heated discussion revolved around whether Captain Gregory had indeed invented nothing.

Lawyer Ellis maintained he had not.

Lawyer Henry Ellis claimed that it was, in fact, an American Indian from Yarmouth who invented nothing during the seventeenth century.

Despite Mr. Ellis's splendid courtroom tactics, there were many inherent weaknesses in his case. Among them, the difficulty to prove anything three centuries past.

On the other hand Mr. Crockett, seeking to prove that Captain Hanson Gregory had invented nothing in 1847, presented for examination an array of affidavits, letters and other documents.

In the course of the debate, the story of Hanson Gregory's life unfolded.

Hanson was born in Clam Cove, Maine, in a charming colonial home overlooking Penobscot Bay.

At nineteen, Hanson assumed command of his own ship, which made him one of the youngest sea captains ever to sail from the coast of Maine.

In that same year, he became an internationally acclaimed hero.

Apparently he had rescued a crew of Spanish sailors from a sinking ship, and his daring on that occasion merited a medal of bravery personally awarded by Queen Isabella.

Yet it was not for his bravery that Captain Gregory was discussed in 1941. It was for an invention which comprised nothing more than thin air.

Debater Fred Crockett, attempting to ascertain the circumstances of this invention, acknowledged the blurring of much folklore with the truth.

Hanson Gregory had not, as some said, invented nothing by accident during a storm at sea.

He had invented it on purpose, as a boy of fifteen in his mother's kitchen.

Mr. Crockett's evidence was sufficiently persuasive to win a unanimous decision from the debate judges. Today, almost forty years later, the Smithsonian Institution confirms that nothing was invented just the way Fred E. Crockett said it was.

Each year in the United States alone, the business which began on a little New England stove grosses an estimated seven hundred and fifty million dollars.

It all started with Hanson Gregory, who noticed that his mother's fried cakes were soggy at the centers.

The youngster picked up a fork, and poked it through the middle of one of the cakes, and invented the something which forevermore would comprise absolutely nothing.

The *hole* in the doughnut.

75. Beloved

He was a handsome young composer; she was an heiress.
To either, the other was "Beloved." And from their oneness
arose like a soaring bird the most passionate music the
world has ever known.

She was Nadezhda von Meck.

He was Peter Ilyich Tchaikovsky.

The love they shared is THE REST OF THE STORY . . .

Nadya von Meck was the wealthiest woman in Moscow,
yet her vast inherited fortune was little solace in the wake
of her husband's death. And so it was, in the year 1876,
that she encased herself in the magnificent mansion on
Rozhdestvensky Boulevard—an army of servants in attendance, the world just beyond her doorstep, yet painfully,
spiritually alone.

There was, however, a piano in the great mansion, and
Nadya was a competent pianist.

This, then, was a salve for her spiritual wounds, the
declarative reply to her melancholy: she played for herself the music she loved.

At the same time, in the city of Moscow, there was a
thirty-six-year-young composer named Peter Tchaikovsky.

Unknown to him, his music was even then speaking
eloquently to the heart of a lonely widow. It was as though
he knew her secret longings and had spun them into an en-
chanted web of melodies and harmonies.

He also could not have known that this woman, because
of her infatuation with his music, was taking an ardent
interest in him personally. From his acquaintances she was
learning his temperament, his attitudes, his needs.

In the greatest romantic tradition, Nadya had fallen
in love first with Tchaikovsky's music—and then with
Tchaikovsky.

At last she summoned enough courage to introduce herself to him. Their relationship was polite in the beginning: "Honored Sir" and "Honored Madame." Nadya commissioned a number of musical compositions, became Tchaikovsky's patron, his mentor—and in time, his confidante, his inspiration.

Thus blossomed one of the most profound and intimate relationships in the history of music, that of Peter and Nadya.

For fourteen years they turned to each other for love in a lonely world, for comfort in sorrow, for sharing in joy.

For fourteen years his most sparkling and passionate music was written for her, and in this the world would owe her a debt of gratitude forever after.

And for Tchaikovsky, the man, Nadya was salvation itself, was at times all that stood between him and insanity.

And one day they parted.

It was she who ended the relationship; some scholars suggest they know why, although no one can know for certain.

Neither survived very long without the other.

Nadya's health deteriorated rapidly, and Peter died whispering her name.

The secrets that did not die with them are preserved in their correspondence. Indeed, that is all we know of them —and all they knew of each other.

For the historic relationship of Peter Ilyich Tchaikovsky and Nadya von Meck, the intense communion of two souls that produced the world's most passionate music—the love of a lonely heiress for a handsome young composer, and his love for her—was a oneness apart.

They, Nadya and Peter, for fear of shattering the beautiful illusion, for fourteen years confined their love to letters.

Never once did they meet.

76. The End

If television, as a forum for talent, chews up the talented and spits them out, it's the nature of the medium.

Even a quarter of a century ago, gifted performing artists were falling from the screen and by the wayside because they couldn't compete with the heavyweights: Berle, Caesar, Skelton.

You can't even remember last season's failures. Could you ever remember this one?

His break came in 1955. The limit of his network television exposure had been a substitution spot for an ailing star.

It had been just enough exposure. The reviews were good; soon everyone in the industry was speculating on the future of this promising new talent.

Within days he was approached by CBS executives in charge of programming. How would he like his own prime-time show?

Trying hard to suppress his spontaneous enthusiasm, the young performer asked what the executives had in mind. Something along the lines of "The George Gobel Show," they said.

At the time Gobel was at the height of his popularity. His format represented what the viewers wanted, fast-paced variety revolving around an amiable central personality.

The young performer accepted; within two months, a pilot was shot for CBS. It looked good—and the fledgling star was signed.

During those first weeks on the air, ratings did not meet expectations. Reviews were mixed. A Gobel imitation, they said.

CBS panicked, called in their star.

The show wasn't flashy enough, wasn't "important"

enough. Starting immediately a string of gaudy chorus girls would greet the audience, would introduce the star; the star would burst through a curtain of balloons, keep it moving; there would be more and more lavish production numbers, replete with fake fog rising from the sets.

In other words, if a Gobel imitation wasn't working—perhaps a Gleason imitation would.

Humbly, the young performer deferred to the network's judgment. And in thirty-nine weeks, the show was canceled. Another "bright new talent" had bitten the dust and dropped into obscurity.

Word spread throughout the television industry like wildfire. He was what no one wanted, a risky commodity.

His agency, William Morris, did not put up a fight. Instead they put him on the back burners, appeased him with vague promises of soap opera roles and such. Next season perhaps; or the season after that.

The not-so-subtle message was there: The End. As far as television was concerned, he was out, through. There would be the second-rate nightclubs or nothing at all.

Somewhere amid the dusty archives which house the history of television, there is a forgotten file drawer full of dreams which went up in smoke. But there is THE REST OF THE STORY.

The rejected suitor for the affections of the nation, the performer who fizzled in 1956, the TV talent you tuned out a quarter century ago—returned to do it his way, to turn you on as have few in entertainment history.

The flop of the fifties, the top of the seventies: Johnny Carson.

77. Siberian Chill-Chaser

The ultimate geographical metaphor for cold is Siberia.

How cold is it? It's so cold—that railroad tracks and tree branches frequently snap off like candy canes.

It's so cold that atmospheric ice crystals sometimes blot out the sun, turning the day to night.

It's so cold that a standard facet of infant education is to breathe only through the nose.

It's so cold that not even a virus can survive in some regions.

It's so cold that the slightest breeze can freeze your face.

And it's so cold—that should you fall through the ice on a pond or a river and leap out of the water to keep from drowning, you would be killed instantly, fresh frozen like a package of Birds Eye peas.

That's how cold it can get . . . in Siberia.

People adapt.

Even at sixty below zero the children still walk to school and the miners still mine and the construction workers continue to work. Life goes on. People adapt.

But wait a minute. Native Siberians are faced with a challenge in addition to that of their own biological adjustment.

There are the myriad *technical* difficulties often beyond their control. Most of their construction equipment is certified by the manufacturer only to forty degrees below zero. At fifty below, electric welding apparatus ceases to function. Period.

For while people adapt, machinery cannot.

That means the people must apply their resourcefulness to their machines; they must use their archetypical ingenuity to solve technological dilemmas rarely encountered by the rest of the world.

In the area of automotives the Siberians have made a discovery which might even benefit *your* car, in the event of another arctic winter.

It concerns hydraulic systems—brakes in particular. And this Siberian Chill-Chaser is THE REST OF THE STORY.

The cold-weather maintenance of their automobiles is of increasing concern to North Americans.

The fact is that most cars have problems at temperatures below zero Fahrenheit. At twenty below and below, no car is impervious to mechanical difficulty.

For counsel, under these frigid circumstances, American car owners are turning to their northern neighbors in Wisconsin and in Minnesota, to people who deal with this inclement climate inconvenience every winter.

As any year-round resident of Green Bay, Wisconsin, can tell you, there is an engine-block heater on the market. You park somewhere, you plug this heater in as a matter of routine.

There is also a portable battery-charger which operates on a hundred-and-ten house current. Another must.

But what do you do when it's so cold that your car's hydraulic brake system is threatened?

In Siberia—where even the slightest breeze can freeze your face—the natives have discovered a brake-fluid additive. An extremely cold-resistant something which invariably laughs in the face of Old Man Winter.

Keeps the people happy too. Vodka.

78. Epidemic at Rozwadow

World War II.

The occupation of Poland.

Thousands of Poles were forced to leave their homes to work in German factories. Periodic leaves of absence were granted.

It was during such a leave that one Polish laborer returned to his native Rozwadow in southeastern Poland. There the worker was examined by two Polish physicians: Drs. Lazowski and Matulewicz.

A sample of the patient's blood was sent to a German laboratory. In a few days the results were issued: "Weil-Felix positive."

Weil-Felix is a test for epidemic typhus.

Typhus.

The Germans had not had an outbreak for more than twenty-five years; the natural resistance of the German people was low.

A typhus epidemic, during World War II, would have been a devastating experience for the Germans and might have immobilized their military, a calamity they could not afford to risk.

The Germans' preventative weapon against such a disaster was early detection and isolation; it involved a blood test known as the Weil-Felix reaction.

When a patient demonstrated the outward symptoms of typhus, a blood sample would be taken and the specimen mixed with a killed strain of bacteria called *Proteus OX-19*.

If the patient had typhus, his blood would form clumps. That is precisely what did happen to the blood sample of this Polish laborer who had been working in a German factory.

Immediately the German authorities told this worker to go home and stay home in Rozwadow. He was not to return to forced labor in a German factory. Meanwhile, health officials would keep an eye on the little town in southeastern Poland.

Soon two more samples were sent from Rozwadow to the German labs, the specimens of suspected typhus victims, and again "Weil-Felix positive."

Apparently a full-blown typhus epidemic was on its way. More specimens from Rozwadow. More positive test reactions. The entire region must be quarantined.

German health officials converged on Rozwadow, confirmed the diagnosis.

The typhus "carriers" were rounded up. Blood samples were drawn by the German doctors, who then returned to their own laboratories to make the final judgment. Sure enough, "Weil-Felix positive."

Thus it was that the town of Rozwadow and a dozen surrounding villages were declared an epidemic area. And while the Germans in six years killed off one-fifth of the Polish population, while they deported thousands of Poles to slave labor in German factories, that region of southeastern Poland was spared because it was quarantined.

Needlessly.

For the Polish doctors, Lazowski and Matulewicz, had found a way to manipulate the Weil-Felix blood test. They had discovered that by injecting a patient with killed *Proteus OX-19*, his blood would indicate that he had typhus when he had not.

And so it was that two Polish physicians with this bacteriological sleight-of-hand spared their region from German atrocities. They saved hundreds of lives and at the same time invented the first—the only—*benevolent* germ warfare.

And now you know THE REST OF THE STORY.

79. Meltdown

By now you know about the Pennsylvania nuclear mishap. This relates to another.

The atomic reactor has gone out of control.

No one at the installation ever thought it would come to this, and as far as I know nothing quite like it has ever happened before—but the worst has happened.

Meltdown.

There is a meltdown of the reactor core.

This much is certain: The core must be disassembled before more radiation escapes, and since the task is beyond the capability of the most sophisticated robot, *somebody* has got to get down there and do it by hand!

No one will volunteer, so someone has been chosen. He is THE REST OF THE STORY.

He is a twenty-six-year-old lieutenant in the United States Navy.

Qualifications: He is highly trained in reactor technology and nuclear physics. He was among the nuclear technicians who aided General Electric workers in the construction of a prototype plant near Knolls Atomic Power Laboratory. He has worked with and at Atomic Energy Commission headquarters in Washington, has high security clearance status.

He is being flown to the meltdown site.

When he gets there, he will study an exact duplicate of the reactor which has already been constructed nearby.

Working with a team of technicians, he will rehearse each tedious step of the dismantling procedure. Television cameras will monitor the moment-by-moment condition of the real reactor.

And then, accompanied by two other technicians from the team, wearing radiation-resistant clothing and armed only with the tools in his hands, he will witness a sight no man has ever seen before: a melted-down atomic reactor core.

The disassembly will be carried out in stages, each a minute and thirty seconds in duration.

In that amount of time, the lieutenant will be exposed to, will in fact absorb, the maximum allowable radiation for a human being for an entire year!

So the economy of time will be paramount. There will be none to spare for fumbling with a bolt or a valve connection, and no room for a mistake—for everyone's sake.

The ultimate fate of this young lieutenant, as a matter of hypothesis, depends on which expert you listen to.

If those who fear the worst are to be believed, then the consequences will far outweigh sickness or sterility, and the price of this mission, for which the lieutenant did not volunteer, will be certain death.

He must live long enough, however, to disassemble the reactor.

And he will succeed.

For the "unimaginable" catastrophe, this then-unprecedented meltdown of an atomic reactor, occurred at a nuclear plant near Chalk River, Canada . . . twenty-eight years ago.

The events we've just related took place in 1951. And the hero of that true story, the young Navy lieutenant who led a team of technicians into the yawning mouth of hell, did not die.

He did risk his life, but he is still alive. In fact, he is President of the United States. Jimmy Carter.

80. The Goat-Man of Juan Fernández

There is a print of a rather detailed eighteenth-century drawing, pastoral setting, the focus of which is a scruffy-looking fellow dancing with a goat.

The ragged character in the portrait really lived. His name was Alexander Selkirk, and he was the Goat-Man of Juan Fernández.

As for many young men in the dawning eighteenth century, life on land was not agreeable to Alexander Selkirk.

Back home in Scotland it seemed he was always in some sort of trouble. Indeed, parish records show that he was cited more than once for misbehavior in church.

In May of 1703, Alex, now twenty-seven, said good-bye to all that, joined a privateering expedition to the South Seas.

Privateers, pirates for hire.

Sixteen months later the ship came to a small island four hundred miles off the coast of Chile. The island was named for Juan Fernández, the sixteenth-century mariner who had discovered it and had tried unsuccessfully to colonize it.

Anyway, there was Alex, twenty-eight years old, the appointed sailing master of the privateer. As the ship was about to leave, Alex and the captain got into an argument.

Tempers flared; Alex gathered his possessions and demanded to be put ashore. He was.

"Now what do you say?" We can still hear him shouting from shore. "You don't dare sail without me!"

But the captain standing on the bridge ignored Alex, issued the command to hoist anchor.

Alex's dramatic ploy had backfired.

Having considered himself indispensable, he was now

wading out to his armpits, calling after the ship, pleading for the captain's forgiveness.

But the stubborn captain had sailed away, never to return.

Thus began THE REST OF THE STORY, the real-life legend of the Goat-Man of Juan Fernández. For the explorer Fernández, upon evacuating the island two centuries before, had left a few goats behind.

The goats would multiply, thrive. And because they did, abandoned Alexander Selkirk stayed alive.

The wild goats provided meat and milk and skins for clothing. Those he tamed became his friends.

Four years and four months would pass before Alex was rescued. He barely remembered how to speak.

He returned to England, became page-one news. Books were written about him, including one by Alex himself.

Thus this comic eighteenth-century drawing. A pastoral setting, trees in the background. And a thatched hut. And in the foreground, a ragged, bearded, long-haired man, dancing with a goat.

For Alexander Selkirk, the imperiled privateer, the Scottish seaman whose temper got him stranded on a dot of soil in the Pacific—the Goat-Man of Juan Fernández—was the flesh-and-blood model for fiction author Daniel Defoe.

He was the original, the real-life, Robinson Crusoe.

81. A Letter from Papa

There is a special pride, as a matter of tradition, that a man feels for his son; for this, his male child, is the direct extension of him, the breathing evidence of his earthly immortality.

And yet there is another paternal relationship, even more abiding and wondrous than the first: the love of a father for his daughter.

When the day comes that he must lose her to another man, the world crashes silently around him. He cannot say so, for fathers are brave. Yet it is so.

What you are about to share is for fathers everywhere who have tasted that bittersweet, who have felt the emotions of joy and sorrow play tag in their secret hearts.

The love of one father, who might be any, is THE REST OF THE STORY . . .

It is the nighttime, and he is home in the quiet, listening to the echoes of years past.

You and I hear only the monotonous tick-tick of the clock.

How long has it been since his daughter's wedding—hours, days? He has forgotten in his remembering.

And though there are no tangible regrets, beyond the absence of her laughter in his home, he searches his mind for loose ends that might have been tied.

Was there a word of appreciation he had not spoken?

Was there an adolescent tear he had not dried?

He can see her even now, a child, smiling, brooding, stirring a tiny maelstrom of feelings in the celebration of youth. Then one day this divine spiritual alchemy of which he was a part produced by its mystery . . . a woman.

Yet in the frustration of the present, sighing from the weight of all that might have been said and was not, this father of the house of the empty rooms will reach out of the night-hush to touch his daughter once more.

In the stillness of that late hour, he retires to his study and to his desk, takes up his pen, and begins to write . . .

> I was so proud of you & thrilled at having you so close to me on our long walk, but when I handed your hand . . . I felt that I had lost something very precious. You were so calm & composed during the service & said your words with such conviction. I have watched you grow up all these years with pride, under the skilful [sic] direction of Mummy, who as you know, is the most marvelous person in the World in my eyes, & I can, I know, always count on you . . . to help us in our work. Your leaving us has left a great blank in our lives but do remember that your old home is still yours & do come back to it as much & as often as possible. I can see that you are sublimely happy . . . which is right but don't forget us is the wish of
>
> Your ever loving & devoted
>
> PAPA.'

Those were the words of one father.

He might have been any.

For in spite of the flowering of human diversity that gives each man his temperament and his station, there is a magical corner of the greater universe wherein all fathers and daughters dwell.

This father, whose tenderness you have just shared, neither sought nor found comfort—in his crown.

For he was the King of all England, George VI.

His princess was Princess, the heir to his throne.

And one day, she came home . . . to Buckingham Palace . . . as Queen. Queen Elizabeth II.

82. Vision Under
a Feather Bed

It appeared to be a great honor, a golden opportunity, when in 1805 William was appointed governor of an entire British colony called New South Wales, Australia.

In many ways it was a rugged assignment, for New South Wales was a penal colony. Still the prestige connected with the governorship seemed vastly to outweigh the disadvantages, the potential hardship and the separation by distance from England.

In February of 1806, William stood in the doorway of his London home, bidding his wife and five daughters farewell.

When the freshly appointed Governor William arrived in New South Wales, he quickly discovered conditions to be far worse than he had imagined.

Corrupt, violent, immoral, the community to which William had pledged his service was comprised chiefly of rum peddlers and rum drinkers. All were controlled by gangsters.

It would take a miracle to restore order there, and there seemed a shortage of miracles in New South Wales, as dramatized by a long succession of previous and unsuccessful governors.

Rum had become a way of life: the colony's food, currency, incentive, all rolled into one.

William's predecessors had either joined the corruption or fought and failed. William sadly regarded his people. They were an overwhelming congregation of prostitutes and thieves, an assemblage of ruthless hooligans almost entirely succumbed to alcoholism. As their new governor considered the near-hopeless situation, he resolved that he would *not* take the paths of those leaders who had gone before him.

William would stay.

William would fight.

William would win.

When it became known that the colony's new governor could be neither bought nor intimidated, the rum-running underworld launched a series of unprecedented attacks aimed at the governor's morale.

William responded valiantly, if unskillfully. In this deep water of weakened wills and organized crime, William was clearly in over his head.

He summarily banned the importation of rum. He smashed the stills which flourished in the area. And at last, embittered by the righteous war of Governor William, the hoodlums decided to relieve him of his authority.

On January 26, 1808, several hundred members of the corrupt military marched on the governor's mansion.

Inside, William went to the window, parted the curtain, saw the sea of fixed bayonets pouring toward the Government House. His attempt to restore peace and decency to New South Wales had failed.

In stolid acceptance of his imminent arrest, he went to his quarters, donned his full-dress uniform. Then it struck him. What if this outlaw militia had not come to arrest and to deport him . . . but to kill him!

Horrified at the thought, William ran to his bedroom, crawled beneath his feather bed to hide.

There in the darkness, wedged uncomfortably between the mattress support and the cold floor, a vision, a waking nightmare: THE REST OF THE STORY.

William saw himself as a captain at sea, being thrust into an ill-equipped longboat by a mutinous crew. Three thousand miles from land, cast hopelessly adrift.

A clatter at the front door of the governor's mansion!

The strange and terrifying vision vanished as quickly as it had materialized.

William broke out in a cold sweat.

Clomping footsteps down the hall.

The marauders had discovered him.

No, Governor William was not killed. He was placed under arrest, was eventually deported, was returned safely to England.

But the nightmarish vision which had haunted him in his secret hiding place, which would continue to haunt him for the rest of his days, was in fact a very real memory!

For once upon a time, William had been a captain at sea, had been cast adrift in a longboat, three thousand miles from land.

And just as the dread dreams of that day would recur, so would the real-life curse which accompanied it.

For Governor William, the man who sought to assuage the ills of a colony, and failed . . . had failed once before.

As Captain William Bligh. The *original* Captain Bligh. The real-life victim of the mutiny on the Bounty!

83. It's Your Fault, Mr. President!

We were at war. Federal spending, twenty times what it had been in peace time. Our President was desperate for revenue.

What he did was to push a bill through Congress calling for more taxes: taxes on estates, public utilities, banks, insurance companies, liquor, wine, tobacco, beef, railroads.

And one additional one: an unprecedented tax on personal income.

This applied to all incomes above six hundred dollars a year, at graduated rates.

So at that time of year when you're digging in pants pockets looking for ten-month-old receipts, trying to compute deductions from mortgage payments and home insulation, fumbling through the remnants of once well-organized records, confronted by endless unintelligible forms, looking around, wondering whom to thank . . . you can thank that certain president. He started it!

Did he imagine, when he started this income tax, how far it would go?

Critics of the Internal Revenue Service are quick to note: graduated income tax is a basic tenet of Karl Marx's *Communist Manifesto*.

And that is so. But in the United States the Communists don't take the brunt of the blame each April; the Democrats do.

Through every Democratic administration since and including FDR's, those with the most to lose in income taxes just can't wait for "that Democrat" to get out of office.

Public antipathy for the federal income tax is stronger right now than at any time in three decades. Howard

Jarvis, godfather of California's tax revolt, is lifting his sights from property taxes to draw a bead on the federal income tax. His announced objective: to sober up the spendthrifts in government.

That particular bandwagon has been rolling all through the seventies. Scores of tax resisters, charged with "willful failure to file," have been going to court. Some are losing, but many are winning.

Some theorists are proposing major reforms of the system. An increasingly popular suggestion is that of taxing at a fixed percentage with no deductions. Under such a system even more revenue might flow into Washington.

If there is a common denominator in this present unrest, it is an aversion to increasingly wasteful and cumbersome bureaucracies, a fear with basis that our American Dream is slowly suffocating under a paper avalanche.

If the Democrats could just stay out of office for three or four terms, some have said, then the complicated systems for which the Democrats are believed responsible would be simplified.

Those critics recall one President in particular, the one who used a nation at war to justify the creation of a graduated personal income tax.

While they are straight on the facts, they have the wrong president.

The man who started it all, the U.S. president who watched federal spending climb twenty times, who sought increased revenue by the first-ever institution of income taxes—did so during the Civil War.

Abe Lincoln.

Republican.

And now you know THE REST OF THE STORY.

84. An Exclusive Affair

Francis Henry Egerton, the Eighth Earl of Bridgewater, was—luckily enough for the sake of his "fine old family name"—the *last* Earl of Bridgewater.

Without his title nineteenth-century Europe would most likely have dismissed Henry as a crackpot.

But because he *was* the Eighth Earl of Bridgewater, and because he was very, very wealthy, Henry was hailed as a somewhat eccentric trend-setter.

Truth was, he wore each pair of shoes only once. Then he had them arranged in rows, so that he could measure the passing of time!

Truth was, he would return a borrowed book by sending it alone in a carriage, accompanied by four liveried footmen!

But the truth was . . . of no consequence.

For Francis Henry Egerton, the Eighth Earl of Bridgewater, was also an extremely learned scholar, a connoisseur and patron of the arts, a fellow of the Royal Society, a donor of important manuscripts to the British Museum.

And an all-around fun guy.

Henry lived most of his later years in Paris, in a grand mansion he called the Hotel Egerton.

Competition for his friendship was fierce indeed! To be invited to an Egerton soiree was absolutely "in."

But there was just one thing that puzzled Henry's acquaintances: Although Henry was known to have thrown the most lavish dinner parties in all of Paris, no one knew just who was invited!

The parties were real, but if the Paris social register offered Henry his only choice of guests—then no one had ever attended!

Of course, the mystery was eventually solved. A team of intrepid upper-crust spies stole away one night to peer through the windows of Henry's mansion.

What they discovered . . . is THE REST OF THE STORY.

Nineteenth-century Paris offered one surefire news service, a grapevine of legendary strength and reliability: the servants.

That's how who's who knew what's what.

It was nonetheless true on one particular spring day when Paris nobility became notified through their butlers and chamber maids that Francis Henry Egerton was giving a bash.

A full-blown full-dress out-and-out dinner party.

Once again, nobody was invited. Nobody anyone knew, anyway.

That was the time when three or four gentle nobles got together and decided to spy! At ten o'clock that evening, they met on a corner in Rue St. Honoré and proceeded stealthily to Henry's estate.

Well within its gates, now, the fearless frocked title-bearers crept carefully toward the grand mansion, farther and farther from the streetlights and into the dark night.

Routinely regarding each other with index fingers crossing pursed lips, they made their way to the great dining room bay. But the window was too high.

Undaunted, foot-to-shoulder they formed a royal human pyramid with a lookout at its summit. As the sentry's eyes rose like moons over the windowsill, he began to laugh, choked it off, rocked backward, and fell to the ground.

For the vision he related, the sight kept secret even by Henry's servants, is recounted by Paris society to this day.

Francis Henry Egerton, the Eighth and last Earl of Bridgewater, the pre-jet jet-setter of Old Europe, did indeed hold full-dress, candlelit, elegantly cuisined dinner parties . . . for dogs and cats!

85. A Christmas Carol

To her fellow Salvation Army corps officers she is Mrs. Major Tanner.

Each Christmastime she is asked the same question by people outside the Salvation Army: Does she really and truly enjoy the seasonal self-sacrifice?

She replies by telling a story which relates to her early Salvation Army experience, a twentieth-century "Christmas Carol" about a doll in a toy store window . . .

Once upon a time there was a family of six: a mother, a father, two boys and two small girls.

Early in the autumn the father was stricken with a back ailment, was unable to continue in his job. The mother went to work in a laundry. Somehow the family scraped by.

As Christmas approached, the parents sat down with their young ones for a family talk. This Christmas was not going to be like those in the past. There would be stockings hanging at the hearth, perhaps even some fruit and candies and raisins. There would be no gifts, no toys.

The children understood the unfortunate circumstances, and they accepted what had to be. It wasn't easy.

The two girls were ten and twelve. Walking to and from school each day they passed the same toy store, and in the window of that store was a doll that especially attracted the ten-year-old.

It wore a blue organdy dress and a lace cap; it had brown hair and it had eyes that would open and shut. In every way it was surely the most beautiful dolly in the whole world!

She realized there would be no presents under the family Christmas tree that year. Still she dreamed of the dolly and stopped to gaze at it in the window, twice each day.

Two days before Christmas a letter arrived in the mail. It was a Christmas Eve invitation to a nearby Salvation

Army center; it announced a special surprise for the children who attended.

Christmas Eve came. Daddy did take his youngsters to the center. And there was a wrapped package for each of the children.

The ten-year-old girl particularly remembered the pretty Salvation Army lady who presented her gift.

The ride home was filled with understandable excitement and anticipation. What if, somehow, the pretty lady had known and had given her the dolly in the window!

Listening to his daughter's naïve expectations, Daddy ached inside. How he wished he could spare her the realities of life, or at least postpone the pain of knowing and growing up.

Yet worlds are turned on childish dreams.

After a long sleepless night and with dawn's early light, the little girl rushed downstairs to the Christmas tree. And she opened her gift. And it was a doll. A doll with brown hair, in an organdy dress and lace cap . . .

The dolly from the toy store window!

This is the story retold each Christmastime by Mrs. Major James Tanner of the Salvation Army.

To those who ask why she so enjoys the gift of giving, she relates what you've just heard, and also THE REST OF THE STORY.

Salvation Army Corps Officer Tanner—*was* that little girl. She joined the Salvation Army and each Christmas, by giving, she's reliving the joy—of receiving that doll.

86. Rescue List

It is easier now than ever before to sue a doctor; rising malpractice insurance premiums reflect this. There are still some physicians who are willing to risk everything in the role of Good Samaritan if it will save a life.

Hawaii, August 1969: a man walking along Waikiki Beach glanced out to sea, noticed what appeared to be a pile of clothing bobbing in the surf about thirty yards out. The man waded in chest-high for a closer look. It was not clothing; it was a young man, floating in the water, apparently drowned. The passerby brought him to shore; the victim had turned blue, had stopped breathing. The passerby pounded the young man's chest, restarting his heart, restarted his breathing.

The rescuer was a doctor.

Malibu, California: two young women were riding up the coast on horseback when a playful dog charged across their path. The horses reared; one of the women was thrown. In the fall, she swallowed her tongue. But someone walking up the coastline that day saw her. That someone rushed to the scene, pulled the woman's tongue from her throat, gave her mouth-to-mouth resuscitation, saved her life.

That someone was a doctor.

Palm Springs, California: a work crew was installing a water pump at a local hotel when a young boy passed the construction site. The boy accidentally touched a live wire; the electricity in the wire held him fast. But a hotel guest sitting on the patio that morning saw what had happened, dashed out, running full speed, tackled the boy, wrenching him from the viselike electrical grip. The boy was saved.

The hotel guest who saved him was a doctor.

I have here a list of nineteen such incidents since the

autumn of 1969. Nineteen certain-death situations in which a physician intervened.

There was the lady in the dining room of a cruise ship who had fallen victim to "café coronary." She was choking on a large piece of Beef Wellington when a doctor, sitting at a nearby table, realized what was happening, rushed over to save her life.

Then there was the cardiac-arrest victim at Los Angeles Airport; he was rescued by an off-duty physician.

And the eleven-year-old boy who fell from a cliff at Rock Point; he was bleeding, dying. The hiker who tore a wrist artery on a jagged rock. The motorcyclist who was knocked unconscious by a car. The suburban housewife who was overdosed on Seconal and Darvon. And the seventeen-year-old restaurant employee who had an epileptic seizure and fell down a flight of stairs.

In each instance, a doctor stepped in, acted above and beyond the call of duty, saved a life.

It should encourage us and perhaps other doctors that in each of these nineteen instances the doctor was *not* sued.

So nineteen people survived, alive and well, because of a Good Samaritan who was an off-duty physician.

In each of these nineteen cases, the *same* physician.

Dr. Max Benis, of Sherman Oaks, California. An allergist.

Now you know THE REST OF THE STORY.

87. Belle

Belle Miriam Silverman was twelve years old and washed up.

Little Belle had enjoyed a rewarding career that had spanned most of a decade. As a child celebrity she had done almost everything there was to do. And now she was through. Retired at twelve.

Tompkins Park, Brooklyn, New York, had had a contest to decide who was Miss Beautiful Baby of 1932. The winner wore a little outfit with a deep décolletage and sang a catchy tune entitled "The Wedding of Jack and Jill." Belle was three.

This was not necessarily the beginning of a carefully planned career, though that came next: singing, tap dancing, piano playing, elocution.

Singled out for her loquaciousness and general precocity at four, little Belle was put on the payroll at radio station WOR in New York. "Uncle Bob's Rainbow Hour," the program was called. Belle stayed with it for four years, using the program as a springboard toward more exposure.

Once during her run on the "Rainbow Hour" Uncle Bob asked, "How do you feel today?" Right there, on the air, little Belle confided her doctor's concern that she might be coming down with the mumps. Every man in the studio raced for the door except for poor Uncle Bob, who was stuck with the responsibility of continuing his show.

When Belle was seven, Twentieth Century-Fox offered her a starring role in a motion picture. In this, the era of child stars with Shirley Temple presiding as their queen, the movies were a part of every little girl's dream. So Belle accepted the challenge, and did very well.

From there it was on to the "Major Bowes Capitol Family Hour," an enormously popular radio program broadcast nationwide every Sunday. It originated from the old Capitol Theater building in New York. Little Belle became a regular member of the radio cast.

And the merry-go-round did not stop there. Belle was invited to do commercials, including the original Rinso White jingle. She also starred for thirty-six weeks in a marathon radio soap opera called "Our Gal Sunday."

Then at last, the moment which comes by necessity to all child celebrities: Belle was no longer a child. At twelve, she had grown to the point of appearing awkward. The sweet little voice was losing its childlike charm. It was agreed by all—Belle, her mother, her father—that a brilliant and happy career had come to an end.

Belle was through with show business, retired at twelve. Subsequent years would be devoted to being just a little girl, before that precious time was gone forever. But there was THE REST OF THE STORY.

Opera lovers today marvel at a glorious soprano voice. To suggest it was once used to interpret "The Wedding of Jack and Jill" or the Rinso White jingle and that its owner was washed up at twelve—surprising.

Yet it's true. For Belle Miriam Silverman, Miss Beautiful Baby of 1932, the child star of radio and movies who resolved after a dozen years just to be quietly simply ordinary, never ever could be just that.

Today she is opera's great friendly lady, Beverly Sills.

88. The Boston Tidal Wave

January 15, 1919, was a warm day for a Boston winter. Almost shirt-sleeve weather.

This is the North End of the city, Commercial Street, Atlantic Avenue. It's almost noon.

The byways bustle with Model-Ts and delivery trucks. Horse-drawn wagons clatter over the cobblestones. Strollers are coatless, hatless, thinking of spring.

Not the slightest warning of what is about to happen. Suddenly, an awesome sound. A terrible rumbling. "Like a thousand machine guns," said one.

In moments, disaster. One of the city's greatest ever. North Boston is about to be engulfed—by a tidal wave.

The torrent tears at everything in its path. Loaded freight cars are tossed like matchboxes. One freight car is rammed right through the wall of the railroad terminal.

A group of city workers are eating lunch at a public works yard, drowned where they sit. Three more workers and several horses, swept into the basement of a freight terminal—all dead.

The tidal wave reaches the Boston Fire Station. The whole building is lifted from its foundation and battered against the harbor wharf pilings. Firemen are crushed, drowned.

Beams of wood and sheets of steel are hurled through the air. A fearsome cyclone of energy unleashed, inundating everything.

A team of horses is slammed through a fence. A sixty-nine-year-old woman is catapulted through a window of her home.

Like the terror-struck inhabitants of ancient Pompeii

fleeing the wrath of Vesuvius, men, women, children—dashing on foot, driving horse carriages and automobiles—try to escape the onrushing tidal-wave wall. They are swallowed instead.

And North Boston becomes a living hell of gasping prayers and ear-shattering screams.

In minutes, it is over. A section of the Boston Elevated Railway is reduced to twisted, dangling steel.

Buildings are devastated, strewn about the landscape. Naked foundations, those not submerged, yawn in the sunlight.

Horse carcasses litter the ravaged avenues, and people too. Dozens dead, hundreds injured.

Where only *minutes* before, workers labored, strollers shopped, children played, is now a scene of unfathomable ruin. January 15, 1919.

Rescue operations, tedious, stomach-turning. Nationwide headlines, eclipsing even those of revolution-racked Russia and the Paris peace conference.

In the six decades since, we have made great strides, have seen many advancements in disaster detection.

Before the hurricane hits, or the earth itself cracks, we can tell—sometimes. Some things are still entirely unpredictable.

Certainly no one in North Boston could have foretold what happened sixty-one years ago: the explosion at the Purity Distilling Company which resulted in a tidal wave of two million, three hundred thousand gallons . . . of *molasses*.

That is THE REST OF THE STORY.

89. The President's Best Man

What you are about to read is a most charming description of President-elect Abraham Lincoln, about to give his first inaugural address. This is an excerpt from *Herndon's Life of Lincoln*, a firsthand account:

"He was completely metamorphosed—partly by his own fault, and partly through the efforts of injudicious friends and ambitious tailors . . . black dresscoat, instead of the usual frock, black cloth or satin vest, black pantaloons, and a glossy hat evidently just out of the box. To cap the climax of novelty, he carried a huge ebony cane, with a gold head the size of an egg. In these, to him, strange habiliments, he looked too miserably uncomfortable that I could not help pitying him. Reaching the platform, his discomfort was visibly increased by not knowing what to do with hat and cane; and so he stood there, the target for ten thousand eyes, holding cane in one hand and hat in the other, the very picture of helpless embarrassment. After some hesitation he pushed the cane into a corner of the railing, but could not find a place for the hat except on the floor, where I could see he did not like to risk it."

Someone came to the rescue.

We emphasize this fellow's presence at the 1861 inauguration, as well as his eagerness to aid the President-elect in an awkward situation, because indeed he was among Lincoln's strongest political supporters and, in Lincoln's own words, "He and I are about the best friends in the world."

Abraham Lincoln's very special friend was one of his strongest supporters in the early stages of his presidency.

It was observed that he was the most attentive listener at Lincoln's 1861 inaugural address.

It was he who was designated to escort Mrs. Lincoln in the Grand March at the Inaugural Ball.

Throughout this extremely critical pre-War Between the States period, when so many of Lincoln's erstwhile friends were deserting him, this particular friend hastened to Lincoln's defense.

He toured the South, begged Southerners not to secede. Even as his words were severely criticized in one forum, he was off to the next, desperately seeking acceptance for the Lincoln Cause.

On extended speaking trips throughout the North—Ohio, Indiana, Illinois—he sought to unite Democrats and Republicans behind Lincoln. And in this he was largely successful. He even won the support of such vehement Southern sympathizers as John A. Logan and John A. McClernand, both of whom eventually became Union generals.

Only three months after Lincoln's inauguration—exhausted, debilitated by his valiant efforts—this very special friend, the President's best man, succumbed to a fever and died.

On hearing the news Lincoln wept openly, ordered the White House flag to be flown at half staff.

Civil War scholar Gerald M. Capers believes Lincoln's friend, had he lived, "would probably have been chosen Lincoln's running-mate in 1864 and would thus have become president upon the assassination."

That, of course, no one can know for sure. But this we do . . .

For one brief, shining moment—in the midst of uncertainty—fledgling president Abraham Lincoln had a friend, a man who supported him, defended him literally to the death.

How poignant the superficiality of history which recalls

these two, Lincoln and his friend, only as vitriolic verbal antagonists. We've heard so much about the Lincoln-Douglas debates, I wanted you to learn THE REST OF THE STORY.

For the man who died trying to promote Lincoln was Stephen A. Douglas.

90. Violin Money

When Joey Barrow was a teen-ager, his schoolmates labeled him the class sissy.

At eighteen, while the other boys were engaging in more "masculine" activities, Joey was taking violin lessons.

All of his brothers and sisters were doing "important" things like looking forward to college, getting married, going into business. Joey's mother insisted he take violin lessons, hoping he, Joey, would also "make something of himself."

But youngsters can be cruel. To his schoolmates Joey was a fiddle-playing sissy. "Joey is a sissy! Joey is a sissy!"

Then one day Joey was called a sissy one time too many. This time Joey smashed the boy who had taunted him, smack on the head . . . with his violin.

It didn't help. Not really. When the story reached the ears of Joey's classmates, it bought him another round of laughter.

But one of the other boys in school did not laugh. His name was Thurston McKinney.

Big, strapping Thurston decided it was time Joey got involved in something with a little more muscle. That is THE REST OF THE STORY.

Thurston exercised regularly at a local gymnasium and invited Joey to accompany him.

As always, Joey had his violin with him. "If you want to work out with me," said Thurston, "you'll have to rent a locker."

Locker rental was fifty cents.

The only fifty cents Joey had was the money his mother had given him for that week's violin lesson. So Joey borrowed some gym trunks and some old tennis shoes from

Thurston, rented the locker with his violin money—and he put the violin inside.

It may still be there.

The first time Thurston invited Joey to spar with him in the gymnasium boxing ring, Joey clobbered him. Flattened him.

The dazed response of Thurston McKinney, himself already a Detroit Golden Gloves Champion, was "Boy, throw that violin away!"

So Joey got to liking the gymnasium. With the money his mother had intended to finance weekly violin lessons, Joey kept a permanent locker.

In five years, Joey Barrow would be twenty-three—and heavyweight champion of the world. There is not much in the anthologies of athletics about Thurston McKinney, but it was he who once upon a time took Joey under his wing.

Joey dropped his last name, Barrow, so his mother would not know it was her son they were talking about in the newspapers.

The world knew for years before she did that sissy Joey Barrow had become the unbeatable "Brown Bomber," Joe Louis.

91. Savior

You remember Alexander Hamilton as our first Secretary of the Treasury. Due to the significance of that solitary title, his numerous accomplishments are frequently overlooked: he devised the federal fiscal system that paid off the Revolutionary War debt; he established a national bank and set the stage for our nation's westward expansion; he encouraged industrialization before its time; during the early years of the United States he was instrumental in averting wars with England and France. In fact, the nation's capital, Washington, D.C., is where it is—because of Alexander Hamilton.

And Hamilton himself would never have lived to make these contributions and he would never have survived the Revolutionary War, had it not been for the young major who saved his life.

In September of 1776 Alexander Hamilton was a captain in the Continental Army, and he was about to die.

Serving under Colonel Henry Knox, Captain Hamilton and his division were trapped by the British in lower Manhattan. Other troops had evacuated in time to save themselves, had fled to what is now the Upper West Side of New York City. But Hamilton and his men were stranded.

Their fate comprised two bleak options: they would either fight and be killed, or surrender and be hanged. They were dead men either way.

It came as no surprise when Colonel Knox issued the order: his soldiers would stand their ground and fight to the death.

In quiet desperation Captain Hamilton awaited the inevitable attack. Suddenly there was the sound of horses' hooves. Were the British advancing already?

No, it was not an army. It was a lone rider approaching

225

on horseback. And the rider was a Revolutionary soldier! But how did he ride through British lines? Hamilton's question was answered soon enough.

The horseman was a young major, General Putnam's aide. Learning that Hamilton and his men were backed into a corner, he sought and discovered an escape route for them. From his own position of safety beyond the British, he had blazed an access to the Bloomingdale Road.

Now, unless Hamilton and his company were determined to die, they must follow the major quickly.

It was an eight-mile march in the driving rain, but by nightfall Hamilton and all his men were safe at Harlem Heights. Exhausted, they could only slump behind the entrenchments and fall fast asleep. But they were alive, thanks to the daring young major.

Alexander Hamilton survived the Revolutionary War. And he became one of our revered statesmen. And surely the face of that young officer—the man who had rescued him—lived forever after in his memory.

He would see that face again.

Many times.

In fact it was one of the last faces he ever saw.

Historians frequently conjecture about how much more Hamilton might have accomplished had he not been gunned down in a duel at the age of forty-nine.

Mostly forgotten is that Aaron Burr, the man who cut Hamilton's life short, and the young army major who spared him even as our American dream was being born— the killer and the savior—were the same man.

And now you know THE REST OF THE STORY.

92. The Woman in White

Folks in and about Amherst, Massachusetts, sometimes called her "the woman in white."

She was small "like a wren," with large eyes and bold dark hair. Her voice was soft, frightened, breathless, almost childlike. And all her life she had lived in the big red brick house at 208 Main Street.

And she wore only white.

In fierce seclusion she drew the walls of her home around her like a coverlet. Except for a few, her secret was safe.

Like many who purposely lead their lives away from the world, the woman in white had become a topic of neighborhood talk.

What did she do all day all alone in the big brick house on Main?

Truth is, her life was as uneventful as the speculation of her neighbors was pretentious.

She was the daughter of a prominent lawyer bound for the United States Congress. Better educated than most young ladies of the nineteenth century, she was remembered by her schoolmates for her quick wit and her comic valentines.

By her mid-twenties most of her childhood friends had married and left town. It was then that she drifted imperceptibly into a habit of seclusion.

Accompanied by her little dog, she often strolled at twilight in the garden in back of her parents' home. To those who watched at a distance this was apparently her greatest pleasure. Flowers and sunsets and solitude, the gentle, quiet, inward existence of the woman in white.

With her father's death and her mother's prolonged illness her uneasiness with strangers became a fear and her fear, phobic.

Then her mother died and she was alone, left to her secret self.

The years passed; glimpses of her were fewer and further between. In May of 1886 the woman in white followed her beloved parents into the hereafter.

No longer would schoolboys stop outside the big brick house on Main and dare each other to knock on the door; no more would the reclusive lady's face be seen through the curtain lace, nor her silhouette in the garden at sundown.

Discovered among her personal effects and private papers were these handwritten words:

> I'm Nobody! Who are you?
> Are you—Nobody—too?

But the woman in white, a nobody all her life long, would posthumously and forever be Somebody. That is THE REST OF THE STORY.

Her private papers, written in the solitude of her room and guarded like a secret journal while she lived, comprised the myriad descriptions of life as she saw it: the tiny ecstasies and candid intuitions, the speculations on the timeless mysteries of love and death.

With language stripped of superfluous words she wrote for her eyes only . . . poems. One thousand seven hundred and seventy-five poems!

This was the secret joy of the woman in white, the young lady irresistibly drawn into her own cryptic self, whose entirely uneventful life was spent in seclusion . . . yet culminated in the immortal art . . . of Emily Dickinson.

93. The British Are Coming!

It was a sweltering August day, and word was traveling like a brush fire through the countryside: "The British are coming!"

No false alarm. The British Army was closing in fast. Looking for one man. A prominent patriot with a price on his head.

In the mounting rebellion against the British, of the small but courageous forces opposing the Crown, he was commander-in-chief.

And he was hiding in a coffinlike compartment in the ceiling of his home!

The secret compartment had been prepared for this purpose. But the heat of August had made it an oven. So, with barely enough room to lie flat in the sweltering, suffocating, starving, thirst-searing delirium of that quiet darkness, the fugitive patriot would try to fight off madness by remembering.

His men had tried to warn him that the British were coming. He had not taken the warning seriously. He had awakened before dawn to hear his dog barking in the yard and the clatter of approaching British troops in the distance.

In minutes the town would be isolated and a house-by-house search would begin.

Fortunately, his home appeared on the official register of the Crown under a name that was not his own. Yet even as he took comfort in that thought, there came a knock at the door . . . the Army of King George! He had ascended to his secret hiding place in the ceiling only moments before.

The patriot's wife let the soldiers in, answered to the alias by which she was addressed. Her husband was visiting in another town, she said. After searching the house, the soldiers ordered her and her two small children to come with them. Temporary headquarters had been set up nearby. They would be held for questioning.

So now the patriot was alone in that torrid tomb, sealed in the ceiling of his own home.

On the brink of unconsciousness he recognized the ultimate horror: If something should happen to his wife and children, he would be left there to die in an unmarked crypt. His forces, leaderless, would surely be crushed by the troops of King George.

Days passed.

No food, no water. The only sounds were the occasional voices of British soldiers taking refuge from the August sun—and the miraculously incessant pounding of his own heart.

On the evening of the third day, when he would almost have welcomed capture by the British, came a tapping at the boards on which he lay. And then he heard his wife's voice.

It was over. The British troops had given up the search, had gone.

The dream for a new nation conceived in liberty—lived.

The fugitive patriot with a price on his head, the hunted commander of the freedom forces, had survived a premature tomb to lead his men to victory, eventually to lead his country.

The nearness of his capture, during those three days in hell, is measured in a coincidence.

The British soldiers, choosing a site at random, had unknowingly arranged their temporary search headquarters in the courtyard of the home of the man they sought!

And that man, who might have suffocated in the ceiling

of his own house—the dissident leader with a price on his head, hiding from the troops of King George VI, in Tel Aviv, in August of 1946—was Menachem Begin.

He is THE REST OF THE STORY.

94. Before the Parade Passes By

Haverhill, Massachusetts: June 1854. At Rowland Hussey's Wholesale and Retail Dry Goods Store business was bad. No wonder!

Not many months before, Rowland had deliberately opened his establishment in a dead section of town. He had said commercial development in Haverhill was headed his way, said his bargain prices and quality merchandise would lure folks from the main shopping area.

It didn't happen. And now Rowland was stuck with a full dry goods stock and fewer than ever customers.

Something dramatic was in order. It occurred to the young businessman that he would organize a parade for the Fourth of July, a parade leading from the cluster of successful shops across town to his store.

He would hire an eight-piece marching band; he would get an experienced orator to make a patriotic speech. Hopefully the pomp and ceremony would attract attention to Rowland's failing business.

July 4 rolled around—and it was a scorcher!

A handful of Haverhill's citizens joined the parade behind Rowland's marching band, most of the others staying in the shade of their front porches, sipping cool cider.

When the band reached Rowland's dry goods store, it stopped to serenade the hundred or so onlookers.

Rowland tugged at his collar.

His scheduled speaker, a fellow from Boston named Wilkins, was nowhere in sight. It was about one o'clock now, and those assembled had been promised a Fourth of July address.

Rowland had no choice. He searched his mind, remembered a speech he'd made as a small boy in school. The title was "George Washington, Soldier and Statesman." That seemed appropriate enough for the Fourth of July, so Rowland stepped up, stood in front of the door of his little dry goods store and made his speech.

Afterward, his holiday audience applauded politely, dispersed.

The parade-as-promotion idea had been inspired, if somewhat misfired. And apparently whatever business Rowland gained as a result was insufficient to save his dying establishment.

It was all downhill from there. A few months later, there was a little sign in the window of Rowland's dry goods store: "Closed."

Rowland went into real estate after his Haverhill dry goods business failed. He might have stayed in real estate, too, had it not been for a friend he'd made, back in July of 1854.

Remember that Fourth of July parade and the speech Rowland made? There had been a certain gentleman in the crowd that day, a businessman named Caleb Hunking. Mr. Hunking had been sufficiently impressed with Rowland's address to remember him when the chips were down.

It was Mr. Hunking, then, who gave Rowland the money to open another store in another city, New York City. And that dry goods business, on Sixth Avenue just south of Fourteenth Street, prospered.

One hundred and twenty years have passed and Rowland's store prospers still. Those who carry on, now that Rowland is gone, have perpetuated their founder's tradition of an annual promotional parade.

Not on July 4, of course. Rowland learned quickly that during the summer, too many folks stayed in the shade.

So next Thanksgiving—before the parade passes by—you'll remember Rowland's first parade in the torrid July of 1854, and that first dry goods store. The owner and proprietor was Rowland Hussey . . . Macy.

Only now you know THE REST OF THE STORY.

95. Death
on the Bowery

It was a routine admission to Bellevue Hospital. A charity case. A Bowery bum with a slashed throat. The derelict's name was misspelled on the hospital form, but then what good is a name . . . on the Bowery?

The admission sheet also missed his age. It said thirtynine; he was thirty-eight.

Someone might have remarked what a shame it was, for one so young! But no one did—because no one cared.

The details of what had happened in the predawn of that chilly winter's morning were of equally little interest to the staff at Bellevue; understandable, considering the proliferation of banged-up down-and-out drunkards who passed through their portals.

Would it have made a difference to those attending him in the last hours of his life, had they known THE REST OF THE STORY?

The cold January sun had not yet crept into the skies over New York City when it happened.

This was the Bowery. One of those rooming houses you hear about, but never want to see.

In one of those rooms was a man, or at least the shell of one. For years he had lived only to drink. Now his health was all but completely deteriorated. And he was starving.

Death would not quite take him by inches, however, for in the loneliness of that predawn he arose from his ragged bed, staggered to the wash basin, and fell.

The basin toppled, shattered.

He was discovered lying on the floor, naked, bleeding from a gash in his throat. His forehead was discolored from the blow he had received falling.

A doctor was called. No one special. Remember, this was the Bowery.

The doctor asked for thread to suture the derelict's wound. Someone found a piece of black sewing thread. That would do. All that while the bum was begging for a drink. An onlooker got some rum.

The doctor shook his head. Nothing more could be done for him here. A police wagon was called, and the derelict was sent to Bellevue Hospital.

For days he languished there, unable to eat.

He received no medical care. Just a bed in which to sleep.

It is remembered that he had a fever. Also that he had lost much blood. Also that he was suffering from malnutrition. But then most of the Bowery bums admitted to Bellevue, consumed in turn by the alcohol they had consumed, were equally malnourished.

On the third day, he was dead.

A friend, seeking him, was directed to the hospital morgue. There among the nameless corpses, he was found.

Recovered from a coat pocket were thirty-eight cents and a scrap of paper. All his earthly goods. At twenty-five cents a night for his room on the Bowery, what money he had would have kept him for one more night.

On the scrap of paper were penciled five words: "Dear friends and gentle hearts." It has been suggested that those words comprised the title of an unwritten song.

For in all ways, this forgotten man was just another of the Bowery's forgotten men—a drunken derelict with no prospects on an irreversible course of self-destruction.

A bum.

Even though once upon a time, long before his death in 1864 at thirty-eight, he made this fickle world to sing . . . "Camptown Races."

And "Oh! Susanna."

And "Jeanie with the Light Brown Hair."
And "My Old Kentucky Home."
And hundreds more.
His name was Stephen Foster.

96. Hyphen Hotel

We've heard about the Hatfields and the McCoys, the Capulets and the Montagues. How is it, then, that we have overlooked one of the most vehement family feuds of all time?

Bill and his Aunt Caroline.

A century ago, Bill and his old auntie were at odds. Primarily because each had what the other wanted and neither would let the other forget it.

Aunt Caroline was the Number One society leader of her day. Bill, by comparison, was a social outcast. As the family fortune was distributed, however, nephew Bill came out on top with a whopping one hundred million dollars to his credit. Aunt Caroline? A mere fifty million.

Until the 1890s, their competition was confined to snide comments at separate gatherings. The inevitable outward conflagration was soon to result in New York City's most notorious hyphen.

Bill had more money, his Aunt Caroline had more prestige; they lived next door to one another, neighboring mansions, with a spacious garden between them.

Aunt Caroline's splendid four-story home was by far the more renowned of the two. It had been built at the cost of a million and a half, plus seven hundred and fifty thousand dollars in furnishings. The third Monday of every January was the most important date on the New York social calendar: Caroline's annual ball, held in her home, guests limited to the four hundred most fashionable, society's elite.

Quite frankly, all of this galled Caroline's wealthier, less popular nephew Bill. For him, in time, next door became too close for comfort. Thus inspired, Bill came up with a delightfully fiendish plan by which his aunt would be forced either to swallow her pride or to move elsewhere.

He would tear down his own mansion and he would build a hotel. A thirteen-story hotel, right there on the site of his present home. It would be the most exclusive, luxurious hotel in the entire nation, but more important, Aunt Caroline's four-story mansion next door would forever be in its shadow!

And it came to pass. March 14, 1893, that hotel, named after Bill, was officially opened: 530 rooms, 350 private baths, 970 employees, towering in its architectural grandeur over Aunt Caroline's comparatively humble abode.

For a while it appeared as though Bill had triumphed. Within a year, Caroline had engaged an architect to design for her a new home farther north on Fifth Avenue, far from the shadow of her nephew's hotel.

What she did not say at the time was that she had plans for the mansion she was about to abandon: it was to be torn down. In its place, to be built by her son, a hotel! A hotel that would be right next door to her nephew's hotel, only with more rooms, more private baths, more employees; it was to be more luxurious, more exclusive, and above all, taller!

To what extent this back-and-forth retribution between Bill and his aunt might have carried itself is better left to the imagination. What's important is that a latter-day Solomon did appear on the scene, in the person of Bill's own hotel manager. It was his suggestion that before construction of the second hotel began, plans be made actually, physically, to join the two together. By operating the two hotels as one, more profit, more prestige for both. And to satisfy the general distrust of one side of the family for the other, every opening between the two structures would be constructed in such a way that it could be bricked up and sealed should the feud be rekindled.

The suggestion worked. A second hotel was built, physically joined to the first. And as a happy footnote, the openings between the two were never sealed.

For what had begun as a feud between wealthy Bill Waldorf and his august Aunt Caroline Astor grew to become a most celebrated name in the history of hospitality, separated by a cautious hyphen: Waldorf-Astoria.

That is THE REST OF THE STORY.

97. Never, Never

The small boy was dead. Not quite fourteen, and suddenly gone.

The boy's mother, overwhelmed by grief, shut herself up in the bedroom. And there she lay, day after day, tormented by memories.

The dead boy's brother, Jamie, was only six. Too young, really, fully to comprehend the foreverness of death.

But the ravages of death upon the living, he could see in his mother. Young Jamie later recalled:

"Sister . . . came to me . . . very anxious . . . wringing her hands . . . told me to go to my mother and say to her that she still had another boy. I went . . . the room was dark . . . no sound came from the bed . . . I stood still . . . I heard a listless voice . . . say, 'Is that you?' . . . I thought it was the dead boy she was speaking to, and I said . . . 'No it's not him, it's just me.' Then I heard a cry, and my mother turned in bed, and though it was dark I knew that she was holding out her arms."

At that moment Jamie was transformed from a boy of six into a young man of singular purpose.

For his grieving mother, he would become his dead brother. In any and every way possible, Jamie would compensate for his mother's loss—even if it meant that he would never, never grow up.

That is THE REST OF THE STORY.

Jamie's brother had passed away and now, for his mother, Jamie, age six, would do everything he could to fill the void . . .

He would tell lighthearted stories to lure Mother from her misery. He would stand on his head with his feet against the wall, "Are you laughing, Mother?"

Momentary distractions, not quite good enough. As

241

Mother was consumed by her loss, little Jamie became obsessed with the desire to imitate his brother in every personal characteristic he could remember.

Jamie learned to whistle just the way his brother used to.

He even wore his brother's old clothing on occasion.

His brother was forever thirteen. So Jamie was determined never, never to grow up.

Intricately the grotesque fantasy was woven. Jamie became his mother's constant companion, attentive listener.

She taught him this lesson: To be a child was to be free from sorrow.

And as the years passed, Jamie resisted maturity with all his might. As though his physical being were joining in this resistance, Jamie actually stopped growing after a point. At seventeen he was barely five feet tall.

In later years still, young children were among his closest friends. And no wonder. Since the age of six, he had idealized childhood and scorned adulthood and the unhappiness which accompanied it.

Jamie, whose youth had become a quest to replace his dead brother—Jamie, who sought eternal youth as a defense against tragedy—never did grow up.

Not really.

You see, Jamie became Sir James Barrie, discoverer of that ageless isle of dreams where little boys remain little boys. Never-Never Land.

Sir James Barrie.

Author of *Peter Pan*.

98. The Man Who Went Out of His Way

Of history's six major epidemics, influenza in 1918 was the most recent.

During World War I, more people were killed by flu than by bullets. In this country alone, within six months of the outbreak, twenty million cases, four hundred and thirty thousand deaths.

In the wake of such devastation, we are inclined to focus on the statistics; we tend to ignore, as a measure of self-defense, the lives of the families which the figures comprise.

Herb Gilbey. Resident of Wallace, South Dakota. By the winter of 1918, the flu epidemic had cast its deadly blanket over the South Dakota prairie, had spread to Herb's hometown.

Now Herb was, in many ways, just an ordinary fellow. But in the bleak season, he was called upon to do a most extraordinary thing in saving the life of a dying boy.

It was the night of the big snowstorm in Wallace, South Dakota, during the winter of 1918. Herb Gilbey was snug at his own hearthside.

A knock at the door. It was Herb's friend, the neighborhood druggist. Herb let him in.

Pale, trembling, out of breath, the druggist explained that his seven-year-old son was gravely ill, was near death.

The boy had caught the flu and there were complications. Pneumonia. He couldn't survive, unless . . .

There was an experimental drug, a new medicine effective in combatting pneumonia. The druggist had heard it was available in Minneapolis, but that was two hundred and fifty miles and a blinding snowstorm away.

He, the druggist, was himself ill. He was too weak to embark on such a treacherous journey. The family's only hope—the boy's only hope—was Herb Gilbey.

Herb knew the druggist's son, the little fellow called Pinky by his mother. For anyone else Herb might have argued that the mission was impossible.

Herb neither argued nor hesitated.

After receiving detailed instructions from his druggist friend, he got into his car and drove off into the cold night. In those days, thirty-five miles an hour was approaching red-line speed for an automobile in good weather. Herb raced over rough rural roads in a dyspeptic, unheated Model T Ford in a blizzard!

But he made it to Minneapolis. And he made it to the wholesale pharmacist. Without stopping to rest, he recrossed the state line and returned to Wallace. It was more than twenty-four hours after his odyssey had begun that he delivered the medicine safely.

Seven-year-old Pinky lived.

Of all the good deeds Herb Gilbey may have done, most significant was this one—during the winter of 1918, when weather and disease ravaged the plains of South Dakota and the life of a little boy was saved.

For not even Herb could have imagined THE REST OF THE STORY that night when he went five hundred miles out of his way. That Pinky would grow up, ten thousand times to demonstrate a sixty-seven-year lifetime of similar selflessness.

You never knew Herb Gilbey.

But now you'll recall that stormy winter night when he cast his own safety to the howling wind, and bequeathed to us the life of a little boy—Hubert Humphrey.

99. Ransom at Whitechapel

Beth has had every advantage, has lived her life in a fashionable section of the city.

Now she is in a cab bound for Whitechapel, a slum, a depth of human existence beneath anything she has ever experienced.

She knows that she is risking her life, and yet this risk must be taken, for she is about to negotiate with kidnappers for the release of a captive.

The men in her family—her father, her brother—have done their best to dissuade Beth from this mission; they have warned her of the danger. But horror stories are ringing in Beth's ears—about the decapitated heads of kidnap victims, returned in bloody parcels to the families who refused to pay.

So for lack of someone else with courage or moral conviction, a woman—Beth—will descend into the wolves' den. Someone she loves is being held in torment, may in fact already be dead. Yet if there is only a chance he is still alive, Beth will take her own chances with her own life.

A man named Taylor is her contact. He is known to be the leader of a kidnap ring, though he professes only to have "connections." This outward role is why the police can't touch him.

Beth doesn't care.

A loved one's life is in the balance.

The cab comes to a halt in the middle of the grimy slum street. Broken windows, filth, tumbledown. This is the address Beth has been given.

At once a gang of men and boys with haunted faces converge from the quiet to encircle the cab.

The danger of which Beth has been warned has become a reality.

And yet it will pass . . .

Negotiations successful, ransom paid, kidnap victim released—exhausted but unharmed.

In retrospect there is no doubt that he would have been killed were it not for Beth. For him a five-day ordeal was over, and for Beth a new life was only beginning.

Within days of this, her first adventure beyond the elegance she had always known, she would marry secretly and run away from home.

And years later, on a sunny balcony in Italy, she would recall the desolation of Whitechapel, the den of kidnappers in east London, the haunted faces, and she would describe it all in a poem so that you would know she was once there—a poem called *Aurora Leigh*.

You may never have read those lines of verse, but you are acquainted with the one who wrote them, the gifted woman whose strict father kept her home until she was forty, the dominated daughter who found her first courage to break free as an angel of mercy—Elizabeth Barrett Browning.

And the kidnap victim for whom she had risked her life in the depths of a Whitechapel slum—the captive indirectly responsible for Elizabeth's first freedom—was never, ever again to leave her side.

A golden spaniel puppy named Flush.

And now you know THE REST OF THE STORY.

100. Act of God

There are only two possible explanations for what you are about to read. It was either the most phenomenal coincidence that ever occurred—or it was an act of God.

Literally.

And remember, as you learn what happened on that rainy Thursday afternoon a hundred summers ago, that a stack of sworn statements and legal documents say that it was so.

There was just one problem with Swan Quarter, North Carolina. It was a lowland town, so naturally the choicest real estate was on the highest ground. In the event of a heavy rain, the closer you were to sea level, the harder you were hit.

A little more than a hundred years ago the Methodists of Swan Quarter had no church, and the only lot available on which to build one was a plot of low-lying property on Oyster Creek Road.

It was far from an ideal location, but they had acquired the land and construction began.

The church was to be white frame, small but sturdy, propped up on brick pilings. In 1876 the building was completed and on Sunday, September 16, a joyous dedication ceremony was celebrated.

That was Sunday, September 16.

Three days later, on Wednesday, a terrible storm lashed Swan Quarter. All day the wind howled and the rain came down in a gray wall of water.

By nightfall, devastation.

Much of the town was flooded; many roofs were ripped from homes by the cyclonic turbulence. The storm raged on all through the night and into the bleak morning.

By Thursday afternoon the wind subsided, the rain all

but stopped. For the first time in more than a day, there was an almost eerie calm. One by one the citizens of Swan Quarter threw back the shutters and peered from what was left of their homes.

Most saw only a desolate waterscape, a community ravaged by nature. But those within sight of Oyster Creek Road beheld the most incredible sight they had ever seen.

The church—the Swan Quarter Methodist Church—the whole building, intact—was floating down the street! The flood waters had gently lifted the entire structure from the brick pilings on which it had rested and had sent it off, slowly, silently, down Oyster Creek Road.

Within minutes, several concerned townsfolk were sloshing about in the street, waist-deep, fighting the rushing current, trying desperately to reach the still moving church so that they could moor it with lengths of rope.

The ropes were fastened, but the effort was in vain. There was no stable structure secure enough to restrain the floating chapel.

And as the building passed by, more attention was attracted, more aid was enlisted. To no avail. The church moved on.

By now the building had made it to the center of town, still on Oyster Creek Road. Then as dozens, amazed, helpless, watched, the Swan Quarter Methodist Church, still floating, made a sharp inexplicable right turn and continued down *that* road, as though the chapel were alive— as though it had a mind of its own.

For two more blocks the townspeople fought the ropes to hold it back, unsuccessfully. And then, in the same decisive manner with which it had moved, the church veered off the road, headed for the center of a vacant lot . . . and there . . . stopped.

While the flood water receded, the church remained— and is there to this day.

Over a hundred Septembers have passed since the little

white frame church removed itself to the most desirable property in Swan Quarter.

In the process of making up your own mind as to how and why what happened happened, you ought to know this one thing more, THE REST OF THE STORY.

The choice highland lot where the chapel settled was the first choice of the town Methodists for the site of their church. And the shrewd, prosperous landowner whose property it was originally turned them down.

But the next morning after the flood—after discovering the church in the middle of his lot—that same landowner went to the Methodist minister and, with trembling hands, presented him with the deed.

101. Fit for a Wizard

The motion picture *The Wizard of Oz* has stood the test of time.

Even today, four decades after its release, if a television station inadvertently cuts a minute or two of the movie, that station may receive hundreds of protesting telephone calls.

When asked to identify the cast, the real names of the actors, most folks can name at least five: Judy Garland, Ray Bolger, Jack Haley, Bert Lahr and the Wicked Witch of the West, Margaret Hamilton.

But there is another actor who receives top billing in the printed credits, right after Judy Garland's name. He is Frank Morgan.

Ten years after his participation in that most significant motion picture event, Frank Morgan died in his sleep. Many of his obituaries failed to mention *The Wizard of Oz* even though Frank Morgan took three prominent roles in the movie: Professor Marvel, the Emerald City Coachman, and the Wizard himself.

What concerns Frank Morgan and the filming of *The Wizard of Oz* seems unbelievable but is confirmed by the surviving members of MGM's staff directly associated with the incident.

It was early in the shooting of *The Wizard of Oz*, during the black-and-white sequences on Dorothy Gale's Kansas farm. Upcoming was the sequence where Dorothy was to run away from home and to meet Professor Marvel, the traveling sideshow man played by Frank Morgan.

The role of Professor Marvel would require a particular

kind of coat: a garment which reflected a sort of shabby gentility, a "grandeur gone to seed."

MGM's Wardrobe Department was notified.

Staff members were sent to an old secondhand shop on Main Street in Los Angeles and returned with a rack of no fewer than fifty coats which potentially filled the bill.

Actor Frank Morgan and director Victor Fleming met to select a coat from the rack.

The one they decided upon was a Prince Albert coat which flared at the waist; it was made of black broadcloth and had a nap-worn velvet collar. The director's stepdaughter, who was present at the time, recalls that the garment was "ratty with age."

And it fit Frank Morgan perfectly!

Professor Marvel's sequence would take less than a week to shoot. Weather-wise it was a rather warm week, especially in the studio under the hot lights.

On one of those shooting days, Frank Morgan was perspiring profusely under the weight of his "ratty" Prince Albert coat.

Between shots, Frank absently turned the sweat-soaked coat pockets inside out to give them—and him—some air.

That's when he glanced down at the lining of one of the pockets to see the name of the tailor, written in indelible ink . . . followed by the name of the original owner, the man for whom the coat had been made.

Skeptical MGM executives wired the tailor in Chicago. In a few days they received a notarized letter of confirmation.

After the picture was completed Professor Marvel's coat was presented to an elderly woman, the widow of the former owner. Yes, she said, the coat had been her husband's.

The tattered garment had been selected because it was right for the part, and because it fit Frank Morgan.

But through what can only be described as a remarkable coincidence—and perhaps a touch of magic—Professor

Marvel, before the cameras, wore a coat which had been made for the original Wizard himself!

The author of *The Wizard of Oz*, L. Frank Baum.

And now you know THE REST OF THE STORY.